For my children:

Reid and Jane who tumbled around the herb garden from the beginning.

AND

With special thanks to my husband Ron for his patient support and invaluable help with research.

DOORYARD HERBS

by

Linda Ours Rago

Illustrator:
Evalina Manucy Stowell

Editor:
Susan G. Knott

Carabelle Books

Box 1611
Shepherdstown, WV 25443

Copyright © 1984 by Carabelle Books
All Rights Reserved
Library of Congress Catalog Card Number 83-062799
ISBN 0-938634-04-6
Printed in the United States of America
Second Printing

PREFACE

Last night I sat in the quiet of the herb garden and waited for a friend to spring up and shout, "Write about me first!" Instead I was overwhelmed by the whole sweet-smelling confusion of sprawling herbs. However, I made an exciting discovery —costmary leaves shimmer at night!

A dictionary definition of herbs ("plants used for medicinal purposes or scent or flavor") is dry and overlooks their full appeal. It surely omits the lore and magic of these fascinating plants. My daughter Jane often goes to the herb garden looking for fairy babies tucked into tiny thyme blossoms. This definition rudely ignores the dignity of plants which have been our attendants since mankind began.

The writing of naturalist Henry Beston about herbs always touches me. His definition of herbs sits comfortably: "A garden of herbs is a garden of things loved for themselves in their wholeness and integrity. It is not a garden of flowers, but a garden of plants which are sometimes very lovely flowers and are always more than flowers."

I have not heard the evening news commentator pronounce "herbs" yet; I hope I never will. It is still one of those words we have the privilege of pronouncing as we like -- as "erb" or "herb." The word comes from the Latin herba with the "h" sound. But scholars for hundreds of years have been dropping and picking up the "h" according to fashion.

A "yarb patch" or dooryard herb garden is as necessary today as it was for your great-grandparents. I do not mean that cute little herb kit your sister gave you for Christmas — consisting of three inch pots of parsley, sage, rosemary and thyme. Those kits have discouraged more people from growing herbs than they have encouraged. Most herbs are gutsy, outdoor plants. They are not houseplants and will not flourish inside for long periods without fancy lights.

Your herb garden does not have to be larger than the "shadow of a bush." Herbs thrive in sunshine and sweet soil with good drainage. You do not even have to feel guilty about neglecting herbs!

Herb gardening can bring pleasure whether it is in a sunny apartment window or in the dooryard herb garden of our old Harpers Ferry house. It is a state of mind -- a year round way of life for me.

The herb gardening year really begins in deep winter. By January the days start to lengthen and herb gardeners stir.

This book contains two sections. The first part offers helpful suggestions for each month of the year for the convenience of new herb gardeners. It is taken from a collection of my weekly columns in the Shepherdstown, West Virginia newspaper, *The Potomac Guardian.* I have attempted to answer questions most often asked by students in my college class on herbs.

In the last part my favorite individual herbs are arranged alphabetically. Among them I hope you will discover your own special herbs to convey the richness and mystery of herb gardening.

Now read and make plans to drink tea from homegrown herbs; to fill sweetbags with potpourri; to make lotions and vinegars; and to enjoy your cooking with newfound, fine and healthful seasonings. And look forward to those exciting evenings of watching your costmary shimmer!

TABLE OF CONTENTS

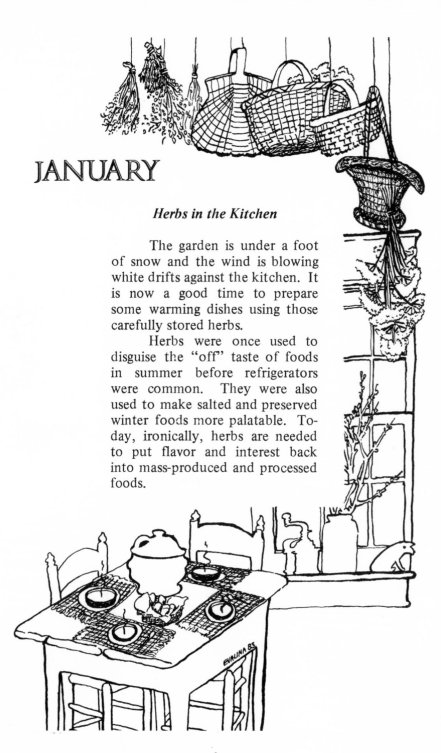

JANUARY

Herbs in the Kitchen

The garden is under a foot of snow and the wind is blowing white drifts against the kitchen. It is now a good time to prepare some warming dishes using those carefully stored herbs.

Herbs were once used to disguise the "off" taste of foods in summer before refrigerators were common. They were also used to make salted and preserved winter foods more palatable. Today, ironically, herbs are needed to put flavor and interest back into mass-produced and processed foods.

As with most foods, the use of fresh herbs is best; however, dried or frozen herbs are much better than none at all.

Do not be afraid to experiment and combine herbs for different flavors. After learning a few basic guidelines in the use of herbs, have fun with them!

A Few Basics in the Use of Herbs

1. Use at least twice the amount of fresh herbs as dried herbs to give the same intensity of flavor. Remember, the art of flavoring is to use just enough to enhance the food's natural taste, not overpower it.

2. Herbs lose their potency more quickly when cut or ground. Therefore, when storing home-grown herbs, keep the leaves or roots as whole as possible. Crumble only as you use them. Buy commercially prepared herbs often and in small amounts. Keep them in tight containers in dark, cool and dry places.

3. Since herbs and spices grown in different parts of the world vary considerably, do not economize. Only buy those which come from the best areas. For example, a friend gave me Hungarian paprika which was dark brown and tasted far richer than our usual red variety.

4. Most herbs and spices yield their flavor readily; therefore, in long-cooking dishes, add herbs for only the last 20 minutes of cooking. Otherwise, the flavor may escape with the steam.

5. Different types of herbs blend best with certain types of food. Try the recommended uses first and then experiment.

Type of food	Herbs
Dessert	Anise, basil, bay leaf, caraway, cardamon, coriander, cumin, fennel, ginger, mints, rosemary, saffron, savory, sesame
Beverages	Anise, basil, bay leaves, bergamot, borage, cardamon, cinnamon, cloves, ginger, mint, rosemary, sage, savory, tarragon, thyme
Cheese, Eggs Poultry	Basil, caraway, cayenne, chervil, chives, coriander dill, fennel, garlic, marjoram, oregano, paprika, parsley, pepper, rosemary, sage, thyme
Fish	Basil, bay leaf, chervil, chives, dill, fennel, garlic, horseradish, lovage, marjoram, mint, oregano, paprika, parsley, rosemary, savory, tarragon, thyme
Red Meats	Basil, bay leaf, caraway, cayenne, chervil, chives, cloves, coriander, cumin, dill, fennel, ginger, marjoram, mints, oregano, paprika, parsley, rosemary, saffron, sage, savory, sesame, shallot, tarragon, thyme
Vegetables	Anise, basil, bay leaf, borage, caraway, coriander, cress, cumin, dill, fennel, lovage, marjoram, mints, nutmeg, oregano, parsley, saffron, rosemary, sage, savory, sesame, tarragon, thyme

Bouquet garni is a fancy name given a handful of herb sprigs tied together and used in marinades or cooked with foods. A bouquet garni includes a bay leaf, parsley, thyme, basil, savory, marjoram, or chervil in various combinations. Remember to remove the bouquet garni before serving.

If a recipe calls for "fines herbes" (fine herbs), it usually means several minced fresh herbs which are added for the last few minutes of cooking or as a top garnish. Experimenting with "fines herbes" is really fun!

Many fish recipes call for "court bouillon," a clear broth in which fish scraps (not innards) have been quickly cooked with herbs and then strained. The larger or whole fish is then cooked in the broth. Traditional herbs used in the flavoring of the "court bouillon" are onion, carrot, clove, garlic, thyme, lovage, bay leaf, parsley, dill, or fennel.

Cooking with herbs frequently and in varied ways should soon become a favorite habit.

Herbal Secrets by the Fire

As an herb gardener I savor January. It is the time to pull a soft chair close to the fire and enjoy some of the best books about herbs. Each year I add a few more herb books to my collection, but like old friends, there seem to be a core of special books that rise to the top of the pile and are enjoyed again and again. Let me share some of my favorites with you.

If there is only half an inch on your bookshelf for an herb book, it must be *Herbs and the Earth* by Henry Beston. In little more than 100 pages, Beston translates the mystical bond between herbs and people into exquisite prose. It is not a "how to" book, but one that makes you hungry to learn more. I read *Herbs and the Earth* each year and always keep at least one paperback copy on hand for lending. The original edition, published by Doubleday Doran in 1935, is rare and expensive. However, there is available a good Dolphin paperback reprint edition.

For those of us charmed by the timelessness of herbs, old herbals are fascinating books. And there is nothing more exciting than using the original sources. Unfortunately, only a handful of scholars can actually hold and study these rare pages filled with the heritage of herbs. Many were written in Latin and the centuries have made them so rare and delicate that universities and libraries make most herbals accessible only for serious research.

Fortunately, winter armchair gardeners can still spend an evening with the old herbalists because many fine books have been written about herbals, and entire facsimiles of ancient volumes have been reprinted in recent years. Thumbing through my ponderous Dover facsimile of Gerard's *Herbal* (published in 1633) and finding the woodcut illustration and courtly description of borage, just as it grows in my garden today, is thrilling.

4

Country folk have passed down herbal knowledge ever since they could communicate. But the first written reference to herbs dates from 1550 BC in the *Papyrus Ebers*. The Chinese herb writings may even be older.

By far the most influential herbal in our western culture was written in the first century AD by a Greek physician and soldier named Dioscorides. He traveled widely and collected the knowledge of the classical Greek and Roman world; his work on herbs became the final authority in Europe for over 1,500 years. The original has been lost, but a manuscript copy made in 512 AD is in the National Library of Austria. An English translation has been reprinted by Hefner Publishing Company in New York.

While classical learning dominated English and Western European herb knowledge, we have one treasured link to the dim past of ancient Anglo-Saxon herb lore. *The Leech Book of Bald* was written in the 10th century AD and it contains herbal remedies and charms that were centuries old at that time. This 10th century herbal has traces of a culture far older than Beowulf; it tells of a time when our ancestors worshipped Eostra, goddess of dawn, and Hrede, goddess of summer brightness. It was a time when grown men believed in water elves and herbs were important in checking unseen powers of evil as well as curing ailments caused by "muckle mark steppers who hold the moors." A modern scholar tells us the entire original manuscript is in excellent condition; the vellum is strong and clean; and the letters penned by a scribe named Cild are still bold.

Pliny was a Roman who compiled over 33,000 facts about herbs and myths and provided a fascinating look at Roman life and herbs. But because he related some wild tales, herbalists never took his work seriously. Pliny was a victim of the volcano explosion that covered Pompeii in 79 AD.

The first great English herbal was written by William Turner in 1568. It was the beginning of a burst of wonderful herbals written in the 16th and 17th centuries. Preceding Turner was Bancke's *Grete Herbal* in 1526; however, Bancke's book was very medieval and covered only European plants.

The most famous herbal, *The Herbal or Generall Histories of Plants* by John Gerard, was published in 1597. His herbal was condemned because much of the book was copied from an earlier work by a Dutchman named Dodeons, but Gerard's richly illustrated herbal is bursting with his own enthusiasm.

5

Dover Publications has reproduced the herbal in its entirety. I never tire of reading it. Gerard had a faith in herbs which was child-like and simple: sweet marjoram is for those who are "given to over-much sighing."

John Parkinson, Court Herbalist to Charles I, wrote several important herb books in the 17th century. He loved a pun and titled one book *Paradisi in Sole* because his name was Park-in-son.

Nicholas Culpepper tied each herb to a star and published his herbal late in the 17th century. The combination of astrology and herbs has always been fascinating. Culpepper made the most of the comman man's desire to be his own physician. The people loved his book, but he incurred the wrath of the medical community. Unlike other antique herbals, an original edition of Culpepper's work may still be found in a musty old bookshop since so many editions were printed. I found a 1741 edition with its original dog-eared leather binding.

Searching used bookstores for old herb books is a pleasant winter pasttime. One of my treasured "finds" is a dusty old copy of *A Garden of Simples* by Martha Flint published in 1900. It is a marvelous and wonderful look at herb gardening from a Victorian point of view.

The 1930's and 40's were great decades for herb books. Some fine scholars and writers in England and the United States were publishing excellent books based on first hand knowledge and using primary sources such as the old herbals. Unfortunately, these books have become expensive collector's items and are listed in rare book catalogues. However, Dover Publication, Inc., New York, is currently reproducing many of them in sturdy, inexpensive paperbacks.

Settle in with some favorite books for your January herb garden. It is the best garden you will ever grow. There are no weeds, no bugs and every plant is perfection.

Why Wait for Spring to Scratch a Green Thumb?

As January goes out, seed catalogues come in. Unsolicited vegetable and flower catalogues are arriving in bunches. For herb gardeners, though, it is time for the excitement of seeking new sources of herbs. Like herbs themselves, small herb farms often have quaint names and come from out-way-of-the-way corners. That new herb catalogue may just have the rare southernwood with a lemon fragrance.

Herb catalogues appeal to the senses. Most are pleasing to the eye - small, neat and interesting with hand-drawn illustrations. Many are printed on paper that feels good to the touch. It may be my imagination, but they sometimes even smell herby.

Always keep alert for new sources of herbs. In addition to herb catalogues, check ads in the backs of gardening magazines, newspapers and herb books.

Send away for herb catalogues to arrive in time for the leisurely browsing of January. Savor them before it is time to get busy with the graph paper and pencil. Because most herb farms are relatively low volume businesses, a small fee will be charged for the catalogue.

My Favorite Herbal Catalogues

Caprilands Herb Farm, Silver Street, Conventry, Connecticut 06238

Carroll Gardens, Westminster, Maryland 21157

Faith Mountain Herbs, Sperryville, Virginia 22740

Far North Gardens, 15621HQ, Auburndale, Livonia, Minnesota 48154

LeJardin, West Danville, Vermont 05873

National Cathedral Herbararium, Connecticut and Massachusetts Avenues, Washington, D.C. 20015

The Rosemary House, 120 South Market Street, Mechanicsburg, Pennsylvania 17055

Sunnybrook Farms Nursery, 9448 Mayfield Road, Chesterland, Ohio 44026

The Tool Shed Herb Farm, Turkey Hill Road, Salem Center, Purdy's Station, New York 10578

Well-Sweep Herb Farm, 317 Mt. Bethel Road,
Port Murray, New Jersey 07865

For a fascinating catalogue of books about herbs, write to Elizabeth Woodburn, Book Knoll Farm, Hopewell, New Jersey 08525. Ms. Woodburn carries everything from new paperbacks about herbs to old manuscript herbals (costing thousands of dollars).

After ordering a selection of herb catalogues, bundle up and walk through the frozen herb garden. Make sure the perennials are still winter mulched. Gently press back any heaving roots. Spring is still a long way off, but you have started your garden.

Herbs Any Which Way

Sleet is blowing down from Maryland Heights. Propped up beside me is a beautiful drawing of Charlemagne's intricate herb garden and a faded old photograph of an English country herb garden at Reigate Priory. The pleasure of herb garden planning is one of the joys of winter. I am planning another small herb garden - the herbs always spill out of the old garden anyway.

Many of us have a limited view of herbs in landscaping - a few clay pots on the windowsill, a row in the vegetable garden or the very formal herb garden of some historic restoration. Open your mind to all sorts of possibilities for herbs.

Nearly all herbs need a light, well-drained soil and at least two hours of full sun each day. After those two requirements are met, herbs do well on their own. They rarely need watering and are practically devoid of insect pests.

Set out several sturdy lavender plants in or surrounding the rose garden. The misty green foliage of lavender provides a lushness the rose bushes lack, and the soft purple of the all summer bloom complements any rose. The combination fragrance of lavender and roses has been loved for hundreds of years.

Include herbs in the perennial flower border. Tall decorative herbs like angelic lovage, woad, elecampane, sweet cicely, bergamot, yarrow and a tall artemisia like Silver King are beautiful as background. Colorful herbs like the annual calendula or chives make wonderful edging plants.

Make plans for your herbs - from the grandest layout to the tiniest dooryard garden. Choose plants carefully and learn about them before the rush of spring. They are the only plants that will reward all of your senses with beauty, flavor, fragrance, softness and heritage.

Systema Horti-culturae
1677 by John Worlidge

FEBRUARY

infusion cup

Oooh! The Pleasure of an Herbal Bath

Now that your herb garden has been planned, pamper yourself with an herbal bath. Fill the bathtub with warm water and a bag of soothing herbs; then slide your chilled dry winter body into the deep water. The warm moisture will relax muscles and mind.

The herbs turn a pleasant bath into a real tonic for body and soul. Use any sweet-smelling herb stored from the summer garden: lemon balm or verbena, thyme, marjoram, rosemary, scented geraniums. Use fresh herbs from the windowsill or raid the kitchen spice shelf.

Tie the herbs in a washcloth or cheesecloth and soak them in bathwater that is comfortably hot. I use a half cup of herbs because I prefer the water at least underarm deep.

Herb lore has long attributed medicinal qualities to herbal baths. In fact, French herbalist Maurice Messegue used foot baths to relieve everything from insomnia to upset stomach.

Comfrey, sage, bay leaf, parsley, and orange peel help skin feel healthy. Chamomile, strawberry leaves and rosemary are said to ease aching muscles. Add agrimony and mugwort to relieve the "rheumatiz."

A favorite old bath recipe to aid a sluggish circulation is equal parts marigold, pennyroyal, and bladderwrack.

Lavender has always been used to relieve tension. Add some meadowsweet or valerian, and the icy February storm outside will soon be forgotten.

Lovage is said to make one more lovable. Add some maidenhair fern or male fern to your bath, and you may find your thoughts turn to romance.

The rich summery scents rising in steam give a sense of well-being and faith that winter cannot last forever.

Indulge! There may be some wisdom in the old Gaelic adage that instructs young girls to bathe in " . . .goat's milk infused with violets, and there is not a young prince on earth who will not be charmed with thy beauty."

The Scented Bower

The practical luxury of a scented garden creates an enchanted bower and provides all the ingredients you need for making potpourri and sweet bags.

Almost all herbs are fragrant, but there are many whose scents are hauntingly lovely enough to merit a special garden. My scented herb garden is nearest a tiny brick patio (or wide walk, as we call it) and a weathered old bench for relaxing. On evenings in June the fragrant oils, released by the hot afternoon sun, rise all around us. My son Reid chasing lightning bugs down the brick paths brushes leaves and releases even more fragrance!

Lavender *(Lavandula)* is the first scented herb to come to mind and the first in my garden. A low hedge of the Munstead variety borders the herb garden on one side. It blooms

11

almost continuosly if I keep the flower stalks cut regularly. Six plants have provided as much as several quarts of dried lavender flowers. Lavender likes full sun and a top dressing of lime occasionally. Taking the advice of a friend, clippings from family hair trims are buried around the lavender for even happier plants.

Pineapple sage is a large fleshy plant whose abundance of leaves gives a rich pineapple scent and bulk to potpourri. The new leaves make delicious garnishes for drinks and fruit salads in summer, and the leaves steeped in grain alcohol make a refreshing cologne or aftershave. My plant rarely blooms, because I cut and dry the leaves regularly, but if left to develop, scarlet flowers appear in late summer.

Those wonderful scented geraniums are also at home in the fragrant garden. I only have space enough for a few, so I try new ones each season. Last year a Rober's lemon rose geranium grew as large as a tomato plant. Tiny lavender flowers appeared as an after-thought, but the leaves smelled just as delicious as the name suggests.

Nutmeg geranium *(Pelargonium fragrans)* is a small low-growing variety I grow to keep the lemon rose in bounds. The spicy scent of the leaves make an interesting addition to herb teas and sachets. Remember, give the scented geraniums plenty of sun and a little richer soil than most herbs.

Lemon verbena *(Lippia citriodoria)* and Lemon Balm *(Melissa officinalis)* grow in the scented garden. Although my bay tree *(Laurus nobilis)* is normally used for cooking, in summer I bury the pot in the scented garden because I have discovered the pungent smell of its dried leaves is a perfect counter point for the sweet-smelling herbs in a potpourri.

Clove pinks *(Dianthus gratianpolitanus)* make a low blue-green mat with tiny flowers like single-leaved carnations. The fragrance is definitely like cloves and the flowers make good potpourri ingredients.

No scented garden should be without rosemary *(Rosemarinas officinalis)* grown in a pot to bring in for winter. Artemisias and mints would be right at home in the fragrant garden too, but they are greedy land grabbers, so keep them in bounds.

A large climbing rose covers the trellis in my scented garden and provides a bushel of fragrant dried rose petels for potpourri or rose jars. I have no idea what kind of rose it is; only that it was planted long ago by another mistress of the house. The garish color is totally unacceptable to rose growers today, and its affinity for mildew and aphids is astounding. It does, however, have a heavenly scent found in few modern hybrid roses.

Thymes are wonderful planted between paving stones or brick in the scented garden. Each footstep releases the fragrance once described by an herbalist as "dawn in paradise." The crushed leaves will only sprout again more profusely.

Specially scented gardens have been planted throughout the country for the blind. Braille markers lead sightless visitors through the unique Smell and Touch Garden at the Brooklyn Botanical Garden. All of us will be richer for a garden that encourages the often neglected sense of smell. One surprised man described a fragrant garden, "It is a cozy garden - like being in a room full of friends, where light is not needed."

The Sundial Belongs Amid the Herbs

No herb garden seems complete without a sundial, the most traditional herb garden ornament. Old sundials are instruments of poignant sentiment, still measuring time by the fleeting shadow. Like the garden itself, time flows quickly over the sundial without the mechanical clicking, bonging and beeping of modern timepieces.

Sundial mottoes are fascinating and most are quite profound. My cheerful sundial is simply engraved with the date 1667, a child-like happy face and the words, "Sunny Hours." Another old dial says sternly, "For Night Cometh." Many of them give prim little sermons: "I am a Shadow, So Art Thou, I Mark Time, Dost Thou?" or simply "Be About Your Business." I like "Sunlight, Visit Me," but my favorite is "Light and Shadow By Turns, But Always Love."

Antique American sundials are almost impossible to find. They were made in very small numbers, and the extant ones are now museum pieces. Most sundials used in this country (until they were commonly replaced by the mantel clock about 1800) were imported from England. Fortunately, old English sundials can still be found in antique shops. Beautiful reproductions are available at large garden stores and most shops that carry brass and pewter. Designing and making your own sundial from wood can be a very ambitious project. My brother tells me it is an enjoyable mathematical problem (not for me).

Because of the retardation of the sun and atmospheric refraction, the time measured on a sundial is irregular. In Harpers Ferry I am told that sundials will be most accurate if set on April 15, June 15, September 1 and December 24.

The bee skep (bee hive) is another traditional ornament for herb gardens. Honey was one of the reasons for growing herbs as the finest honey often came from the herb garden bees. A rye straw bee skep will deteriorate if left outside all year. Remember, build a small shelter or bring it inside during a storm.

Birdbaths in the herb garden are excellent focal points if they are simple and blend with the herbs in size and color. The type of birds lured will make a healthier and more cheerful garden. Black iron kettles are effective as bird baths in a kitchen herb garden.

One special ornament is usually enough for a small herb garden - so enjoy the search for just the right one!

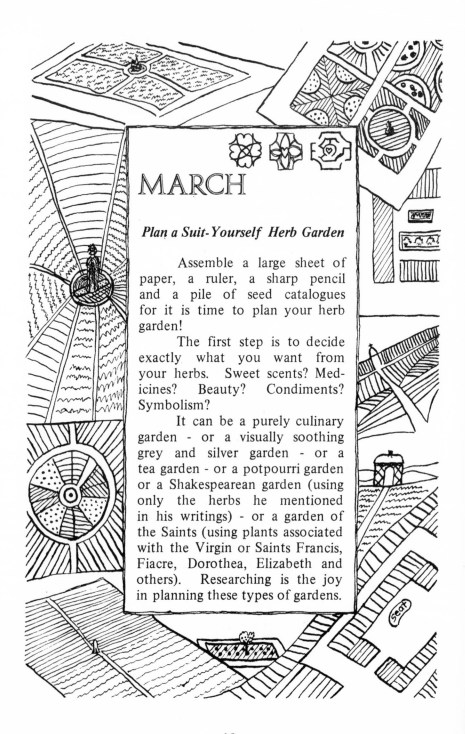

MARCH

Plan a Suit-Yourself Herb Garden

Assemble a large sheet of paper, a ruler, a sharp pencil and a pile of seed catalogues for it is time to plan your herb garden!

The first step is to decide exactly what you want from your herbs. Sweet scents? Medicines? Beauty? Condiments? Symbolism?

It can be a purely culinary garden - or a visually soothing grey and silver garden - or a tea garden - or a potpourri garden or a Shakespearean garden (using only the herbs he mentioned in his writings) - or a garden of the Saints (using plants associated with the Virgin or Saints Francis, Fiacre, Dorothea, Elizabeth and others). Researching is the joy in planning these types of gardens.

For a first herb garden, you may prefer a little of everything. Half of my garden is cooking herbs, the other half is sweet-scented herbs and the border is symbolic or medicinal herbs.

Go slowly at first. It is a mistake to grow too many varieties, for each plant is an individual presence and there is pleasure in knowing each one well.

A dozen of my favorites for a first-time garden include basil, thyme, rosemary, hyssop, lavender, rue, sweet marjoram, lemon balm, oregano, sage, bergamot, and calendula. They are all easy to work with; give an idea of the joy herbs can bring to gardening and living; and their history is long and fascinating.

The next step is to choose a spot for planting the herbs. Some gardeners like to include herbs in the flower beds or use them as companion planting among vegetables. The herbs do well and look pleasing, but the tranquility and form of a tiny garden of only herbs is one of its greatest joys. A gangling tomato plant or a hot pink zinnia flower belong elsewhere.

Herb gardens should ideally be enclosed within a fence to give them definition and protection from wind. A wall is always useful, too. The el of the house or an outbuilding is perfect. Either informal plantings or geometric beds are fine if pathways are wide enough and planting areas small enough to cultivate easily.

The southwest side of our house and the southern garage wall make a perfect protected el for my garden. A neat white picket fence closes the two open sides and gives definition to the space. My husband Ron made geometric paths and a tiny terrace from hand-made Harpers Ferry brick. Sun-warmed bricks in the old house hold their heat and make a cozy place for heat-loving herb plants. The garden is private and serene--the way an herb garden should be.

But if space is limited, grouping pots of herbs near the door can be your own special herb garden. The Italians have a wonderful name for these tiny tucked-away gardens - I Giardinetti.

A small cottage in Harpers Ferry is tucked into the hill near the old Harper Cemetery. Herbs and flowers spill over the stone walls and nestle every which way around the little house. The tidy garden-keeper is a retired lady who never lets you say good-bye without a slip of some old-time plant in your pocket. It is my favorite garden in which to poke about! Two apple mint plants will surprise you by the front door, and then you notice a tiny mother-of-thyme creeping from beneath an old wooden tub of pepper plants. Each inch of space is gardened, and the visual effect is breath-taking.

Sunshine, good drainage and reasonable soil are necessary. If your sun is limited, some herbs like mint, tarragon, chervil, or sweet woodruff tolerate more shade.

Make your herb garden a special place. One where the herbs, as one herbarist wrote, will let you hear " . . . in the full of one's own peace, the serene footsteps of the year."

The plan is the start. Stand outside and visualize the garden. When spring arrives, the realities of proper soil and drainage may alter your plans. The first step has been taken and you now have an herb garden.

And as 17th century John Parkinson said, "To prescribe one form for every man to follow were too great presumption and folly: for every man will please his own fancie."

Learn From Others

One of the best ways to learn about herbs is to often share ideas and mistakes with other herb growers. Seeing another herb garden can trigger a thousand ideas for your own. Recently another herb gardener passed along her solution to a drainage problem - dig a small dry well in the middle of her herb patch. And a lady from Virginia shared with me her source for the low acidic herb garden mulch, cocoa hulls - special order from Southern States Cooperative.

Plan to make a few spring excursions to nearby herb gardens. Top on your list should be the new National Arboretum Herb Garden in Washington, D.C. It has over an acre of herbs with a knot garden and specialty gardens for medicines, dyes, teas, bees and many more. All are carefully labeled and the uses are explained.

Another herb garden open to the public is the Bishop's Garden at the Washington Cathedral in Washington, D.C. It has a small medieval garden with a lovely 9th century font. There is also a greenhouse with herb plants for sale.

In Annapolis, Maryland, there is a small 18th century herb garden planted at the Spicer Shiplap House off Market House Square near the wharf. Not far away in Ephrata, Pennsylvania is the restored Ephrata Cloister built before 1749. The herb garden is typical of the type planted by early German settlers; it is a little different from the usual English design.

In Virginia, of course, is the kitchen garden at Mount

Vernon. Williamsburg has many herb gardens, and Monticello near Charlottesville has herbs growing in the vegetable garden. Belle Grove Plantation near Middletown, Virginia, is a fine example of an early informal farm herb patch.

Morgan Cabin near Bunker Hill, West Virginia, has a little dooryard planting of herbs that an early log cabin settler might have grown.

In Harpers Ferry, you are always welcome to peek over the picket fence at my garden - just pull a weed as you leave!

Seedlings on the Windowsill

Although March often comes in like a lion here in the Blue Ridge, the sun now spreads deeper into my kitchen as it settles over Bolivar Heights. Only a few weeks of winter are remaining. Spring is only weeks away and for many the urge to begin the herb garden is much too strong.

So now is the time to start seeds indoors. Find the coolest, sunny window. Try such annual herbs as basil, summer savory, chervil, calendula and sweet marjoram. With patience, perennial herbs such as hyssop, salad burnet, chives, fennel, penny-royal, sage and thyme will grow from seed.

Basil will grow from seed sown indoors, and it transplants well outside when the ground is warm without chance of night frost. However, I have discovered that basil seeds sown outside about the same time inside basil is planted often catch up in a few weeks. It is almost impossible to give basil seedlings enough light indoors, and they must be hardened off gradually.

Dill and parsley are almost impossible to grow successfully from seed indoors to be planted outside later. Parsley has a long tap root that refuses to be moved and dill has such a delicate root structure that it never really recovers the shock of a transplant. Dill grows nicely, though , when sown outside in April. In fact, plants sown outside are usually bushier.

Herbs that are difficult to grow from seed include angelica, tarragon, most artemisias, santolina, germander, mints, rosemary, and lavender. Most of these herb seeds are so fine, the seedlings so delicate and the germination period so long (up to six months) that patience will wear thin. I have a half-inch self-sown rosemary seedling growing in the pot with a large rosemary which has not set seed since August.

For early indoor planting, fill flats or pots with a very

18

fine mixture of two parts sand and one part vermiculite. Moisten the growing mixture and sow the seeds thinly.

Most tiny herb seeds need only be pressed slightly; do not cover with soil. Keep them in a place with good light and water them from the bottom. As soon as the seeds sprout, move them to the sun. They will need night temperatures of 50° to 60° F. and fresh air during the day. When the seedlings have several leaves and look sturdy, transplant them to pots with good garden loam and apply compost or peatmoss.

Late in March or early April, harden off the seedlings by grouping them together in a protected spot outdoors for a few days. Be sure to bring them inside if there is a cold spell, or if the seedlings begin to look a little sad. Soon you will notice a healthy outdoor look to them, and they will be ready for the garden.

Getting through March is necessary before gardening can begin in earnest. Meddling or cursing is not of any use, and planting seeds indoors only helps us feel a little better. During March, 'tis best to just keep muttering, "Patience is the mother of wisdom."

Deep Digging

Toward the end of March the soil often dries out enough for the first outdoor herb gardening job. If a handful of dirt from the garden crumbles when squeezed, it is time to till.

Preparing the soil for the herb garden starts with deep digging. After a spot has been chosen, mark off the boundaries of the plot with lime just a little larger than the size of the actual beds. Then dig up the entire area at least twelve inches deep.

Raking out stones and roots is an essential next step. If the herb garden has always been a grassy spot, you will never regret sifting out as many grass roots as possible. I always become impatient and tend to leave too many roots; consequently, I pay dearly by spending many hours pulling up witchgrass all summer.

The third step is to add a two-inch layer of compost or rotted manure. Mix it in thoroughly. Cow manure is best, but horse or rabbit manure works well too. Be generous now and fertilizer may not have to be added to the herb garden for several years. Established perennial herbs are most aromatic on poorer soil, but young plants and seedlings seem to prefer a rich soil.

The next step is to dust the garden with a fairly heavy layer of lime. The earth should be almost white. If your soil already has a pH of 7.0 or higher the lime can be omitted initially; however, remember to sprinkle a little lime over the garden every two or three years to keep the soil sweet. Most herbs like an alkaline soil and even the ones which like a little more acidic soil will tolerate the lime.

Now is the time to make curving stone paths in an informal herb garden. These paths add visual interest and give space to the gardener to weed and harvest the herbs. Once the beds are cultivated, do not walk on them as the soil will become compacted. Brick or mulched paths are good for either an informal or formal geometric garden. Grass paths seem to wander over into the garden and make weeding very difficult.

Raised beds are perfect for herb gardening - especially if drainage is less than perfect. Border beds with boards, bricks or stones several inches higher than the soil level. Add enough compost and good top soil to fill the beds. Do not use boards or railroad ties treated with creosote; the nasty smell of creosote will overpower the delicate fragrance of the herbs.

Water the freshly cultivated garden thoroughly a day or two before sowing seeds or setting out the herb plants. Most herbs should not go in the garden until the middle of April, but lavender and borage seed can be planted successfully in the fall.

Parsley is traditionally planted on Good Friday since it takes so long to germinate. Folklore has it that parsley seed must go to the devil and back three times before it will germinate. Why not cheat the devil out of at least several trips by soaking the parsley seed overnight in warm water before sowing it?

APRIL

At Last !!

During the early weeks of April, I lift the winter mulch of hay and Christmas tree boughs from perennial herbs and then let them fall back again. Silvery little artmeisia shoots and tightly pleated bergamot leaves are appearing, but they are now most vulnerable to a hard frost.

On a cloudy day early this month, I shall take off the winter cover gradually so that the new herb growth will not sunburn. It is the time to divide or transplant crowded clumps of chives or tarragon or others.

I always regret failing to mark perennial herbs in the fall. Invariably the bare spot I have chosen for a new costmary will be full of forgotton sweet cicely roots.

Label! Mark not only the spots in the herb garden where the seeds have been sown, but maintain sturdy identification markers for established herbs. You will learn the botanical names as well as the common names; it will make garden maintenance easier; and visitors will enjoy the herb garden so much more.

Separate perennial and annual herbs. Since spots for annual herbs must be dug up each spring, it is best to provide a bed just for them. Perennial roots do not want to be disturbed each year.

Rake the annual beds and water them thoroughly several hours before sowing herb seed. Read the labels on seed packets carefully and follow the directions for depth of covering and time for sowing. If in doubt, err on the side of too little depth in covering seeds. Very fine herb seeds like marjoram or basil need to be pressed into the soil until just out of sight. Keep the beds moist until the seeds sprout. Herbs slow to germinate such as lemon balm, marjoram, and parsley will come up much sooner if they are soaked overnight in lukewarm water.

Some perennial herbs like lavender or rosemary take so long to germinate and are so slow growing that by fall they are only a few inches high and may easily be winter-killed. I recommend buying well-potted plants to start your garden. By late summer they will be sturdy enough for you to take several stem cuttings for more plants next year.

Choose compact plants with healthy new growth and treat them fairly. Dig a deep and wide hole. Fill it with water and then let the water drain out. Gently lift the plants from their pots and dip them in a pail of lukewarm water. Shake the roots up and down untangling them so they can stretch down into the soil. Then carefully set the plant in the hole, spread out the roots and tuck in the soil around it. Firm the soil gradually as the hole is filled, but never press hard enough to damage the roots. Keep the new transplant under an upturned basket or flowerpot for several days to protect it from the sun. Each evening water the plant and remove the cover.

Now stand back and watch the herbs flourish. Weeding and mulching come later. For the present just visit the garden each morning and watch each tiny leaf uncurl toward the sun. Savor the unique beauty of each herb as it fulfills its heritage of soothing, flavoring, scenting, protecting or healing.

A Spring Tonic

The spring tonic was once an annual event for country folk. If looking a little peaked from the long winter, a tonic was the sure remedy. Grandmother claimed a tonic would increase the appetite, improve the circulation and make you feel healthy and robust.

Of course, there were the vile tasting patent medicines like Stonebraker's Blood and Liver Bitters called the "great Blood Purifier and Liver Invigorator" or Warner's Log Cabin Sassaparilla, a "roots and herbs preparation" advertised as a purifier and tonic. More often, though, the first green plants to come up were brewed into tonics, according to recipes handed down from mothers and grandmothers.

In my own family the earliest watercress *(Nasturtium nasturtium-aquaticum)* was eagerly gathered and eaten long before the garden provided greens. The bitterness of cress was valued as an appetite stimulant. Catnip tea brewed from the newest green leaves in spring was another of my own West Virginia grandmother's specialities.

Amish children in Pennsylvania still pick the early violet flowers and nibble them with as much relish as a lollipop. Both the leaves and flowers of violets are rich in Vitamin C. After a winter diet of very few fresh vegetables, violets would indeed be a tonic for the body as well as the spirit.

Tansy is an aromatic, bitter herb often used as a weak tea for tonic. Yarrow was one of the most widely used plants in tonic recipes.

Chicory and its relative, dandelion, were said to be good plants for a spring tonic; southern Europeans have been using them for centuries to increase the appetite.

Fresh horehound tea is another nutritious tonic, although its most well-known use is as a cough remedy. One of the oldest tonics is chamomile; however, since the flowers are not blooming in early spring, it must have been a summer tonic.

Mint, wild ginger, wormwood, sweet fern fiddleheads and bee balm (bergamot) are traditional spring tonic plants. Brew them into a light tea.

Why not ask elderly friends or family members to recall recipes or plants used as tonics? If it is not possible to brew up a traditional spring tonic, sit down with a symbolic tonic of gingerale with a sprig of fresh mint. Get those juices flowing!

Take a Lesson from the Mandrake

There are thousands of herbs claimed by some to have powers of healing and almost as many books describing herbal cures for every human malady. In the past decade many of us have re-discovered the pleasures of herb teas and fragrances, and some of us have scrambled to find natural herb medicines to treat serious illness. It is true that some herbs are powerful medicines, but it is often difficult to draw the line between medicine and magic.

Our ancestors attributed almost as much power to the rites and incantations used while gathering and preparing herbs as to the plants themselves. Today the most powerful medicine men are those who come out with the latest best-seller touting an instant cure, herbal or otherwise, for obesity, depression or the "sagging economy." Is it any less magic for being modern? Are we country folk any less gullible?

The height of herbal superstition was reached with the mandrake *(Mandragora officarum)* whose root is valued because it often grew in the shape of a man or woman. (Today none of us would be able to recognize the plant, but the name is recognized by most.) Since the time of Aristotle, mandrake root has been accorded mystical power, but in truth the root was often carved to resemble the human body.

Throughout the Middle Ages mandrake was highly valued as a painkiller; and therein a shred of truth may lie because the plant does seem to contain an alkaloid which can cause hallucinations.

Over the centuries dozens of grotesque legends developed about the mandrake. For example, to dig up a root a circle must be drawn around the plant with a sword and the digging accomplished only with a favorable wind. Or a dog must be tied to the root to pull it out so that evil would befall the dog instead of the human. The strangest and most widely known belief was that the mandrake root shrieked like a human when torn from the earth.

Lawyers, take note: a mandrake root tucked in the right armpit of a claimant in a law suit guarantees its successful issue.

Shakespeare and his audiences were aware of the wonder and mystery of the mandrake. Juliet feared that when she awakened in the tomb she would shriek "like Mandrakes torn out of the earth." Cleopatra cried, "Give me to drink Mandrake. . .That I might sleep out this great gap of time . . . My Anthony is away."

Because of its human form and the belief that mandrake was the herb of the Old Testament story in which Rachel conceived a child, mandrake was used to cause "unfruitful women to bear." These uses must have been interesting because in 1633 the herbalist Gerard wrote of mandrake ". . .in loving matters, too full of scurrilitie to set forth in print."

Skepticism about the miraculous mandrake is almost as old as the fable; even one of Aristotle's pupils teased the herb-gatherers about mandrake. Many of the well-known herbalists ridiculed it; and in the 13th century one writer recounted the mandrake legends and then said, "It is so feined with churles."

Savor the sweetness of your herbs, enjoy their healthful goodness, but remember the mandrake and chuckle when you are tempted to try a "miraculous cure" of the modern medicine man.

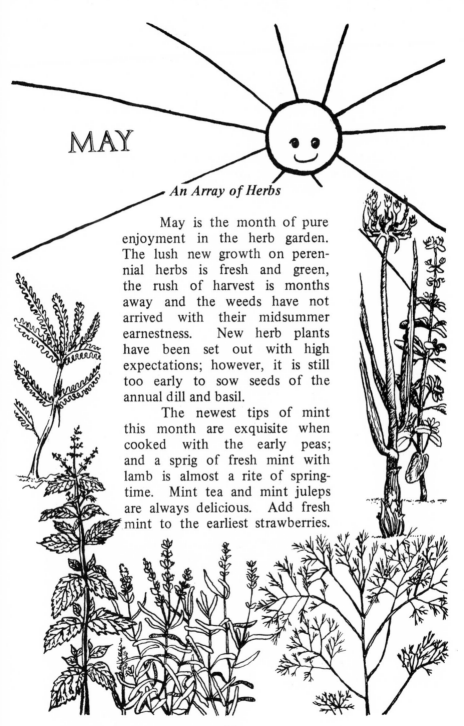

MAY

An Array of Herbs

May is the month of pure enjoyment in the herb garden. The lush new growth on perennial herbs is fresh and green, the rush of harvest is months away and the weeds have not arrived with their midsummer earnestness. New herb plants have been set out with high expectations; however, it is still too early to sow seeds of the annual dill and basil.

The newest tips of mint this month are exquisite when cooked with the early peas; and a sprig of fresh mint with lamb is almost a rite of springtime. Mint tea and mint juleps are always delicious. Add fresh mint to the earliest strawberries.

Chives are ready to use by May; the first tender stalks are the most flavorful. Fresh chives excite me so that in May I begin adding them to everything: omelettes, salads, cottage cheese, sour cream, butter, bread. . . . .

That wonderful salad herb, salad burnet, often stays green throughout the winter, and by May it has sprouted new growth. These delicate leaves give the taste of real cucumber to the first spring salads of spinach and leaf lettuce.

Combine several herbs from the May herb garden in this delicious recipe for Spring-Green Spread taken from the files of a fellow herb gardener in Connecticut.

Adelma Simmon's Spring-Green Spread

A three ounce package of cream cheese
2 tablespoons chopped chives
4 tablespoons finely chopped burnet leaves
¼ cup chopped lettuce
2 tablespoons dry white wine
Salt and Pepper

Blend all of the above ingredients. Let the mixture stay in the refrigerator overnight before using.

By May the tarragon is no taller than the nearby creeping sweet woodruff, but the leaves are already curling like the little dragons that fostered its name. The world is divided into those who love anchovies and those who hate them. For the lovers, a combination of tarragon and anchovies is wonderful. Try this recipe.

Anchovies and Tarragon Spread

A six ounce package of cream cheese
A two ounce can of anchovies
2 new sprigs of tarragon
1 teaspoon chopped chives

Combine the above ingredients and serve on crackers or toast.

Lemon balm and beebalm leaves are usually up several inches in May and are ready for the teapot, the tiniest borage leaves are ready for the salad bowl and new oregano leaves are ready for the pizza. Lovage is already a foot tall and waiting for a few leaves to be chopped in a tuna fish salad.

The usually grey lavenders are clear green only in May; stately southernwood is almost delicate in May. The new clumps of yarrow look like bright green feather dusters all in a row.

These May pleasures of the herb garden should not be missed. Enjoy the early lull before setting out tender new herb plants, sowing annual herbs, and attacking weeds. Renew your acquaintance with the fragrant herbs. Not a trace of winter is left!

Herbal Trees

A dogwood tree stands watch over the northern end of my herb garden where it provides shade for tarragon and sweet woodruff. Pots of new seedlings or cuttings find green protection from the sun under its drooping branches. Its leaves have unfolded now and it will be the perfect background for scarlet roses, bright lavender, and calendula. It is a reminder that many trees are traditionally "herb trees" and that every herb garden should include at least one such tree.

The dogwood bark was brewed into a spring tonic tea by Indians and early settlers. Tender tips of hemlock trees, black and red spruces were also made into medicinal teas by Indians and French settlers.

Holly trees planted outside the house were thought to insure it from dangers of the "Evil Eye," fire and storms. The red berries discouraged witchcraft. Cow's milk was said to improve if a sprig of holly from church decorations were hung in the barn.

Juniper trees were most honored in England. Branches were burned to drive away fleas, to prevent infection from spreading or to keep out witches. Oak and yew trees were also thought to protect the house from witches; a concoction of oak leaves was thought to cure one of gout.

The hazelnut tree was a symbol of fire and fertility to the Celts. Even today those who profess the ability to locate underground water by divining rod prefer hazelwood sticks. In Wales hazel twigs worn in the hair would give you the desire of your heart. Maidens could determine their future husband by placing hazelnuts in the embers of the fire and whispering the name of suitors. When the future husband's name was whispered, the hazelnut would jump.

Elder trees were the symbol of sorrow and death and were said to harbor an evil spirit. Superstitious gardeners would often refuse to trim elder trees. Gypsies would never gather elder wood for their campfires in fear of offending the evil spirit.

Aspen trees were thought to cure a shivering fever by pinning a shred of bark in the sufferer's hair and saying, "Aspen tree, aspen tree, I prithee to shake and shiver instead of me."

The pretty mountain ash or rowan tree, bearing orange berries in the fall, protects the house by which it grows. A rowan leaf in the pocket protects one from rheumatism; and a twig in the butter churn prevents the butter from turning sour. The bark was brewed into a tea to cure fever and malaria. In Europe branches were brought into the house on Good Friday to bless the house for the coming year.

Sassafras roots and sumac berries *(Rhus glabra)* make delicious beverages. Many trees make colorful dyes.

Include at least one herb tree in your garden and take pleasure in its usefulness or fascinating heritage.

JUNE

Herbs for a Happy Marriage

This is the month of romance and weddings. Herbs have been entwined with wedding rituals for thousands of years. Romantic wedding feasts are the time for herbs to take their traditional place in wishing the wedding couple all the good things in life.

A bridal bouquet should include a sprig of sage to insure domestic peace, good health and long life; a sprig of lavender for undying love; jasmine for peace; marjoram, the gypsy herb of love; and borage the symbol of courage. Always borage!

Rosemary is the true medieval wedding herb. In preparation for the wedding ceremony the church and household were decorated with rosemary. Brides and bridesmaids carried rosemary branches tied with gilded ribbons to signify constancy, fidelity, loyalty, and enduring love.

The classical wedding herb is the hawthorne, an emblem of hope. Ancient Greek brides carried hawthorne blossoms on their wedding day; the altar of Hymen, God of Marriage, was lighted by torches of hawthorne. Even the bridal chamber was lit by hawthorne.

The linden tree and blossoms were another ancient Greek wedding herb from the legend of Philimon and Baucis. It is the symbol of conjugal love.

Although many liberated brides carry the traditional orange blossoms, they would be surprised to know it is the symbol of fecundity. Orange blossoms represented a pagan appeal to the orange tree spirit that the bride bear many children.

Rue, the symbol of virginity, had a special use at Eastern European weddings where both bride and groom wore crowns of rue to represent good health and long life.

Herbal wedding presents were common in the past. Would it not be a nice custom to revive? A broom plant for the couples garden represents ardor and humility - necessary for any good marriage. Honesty *(Lunaria)* or the money plant was often given to couples for their new garden; thus keeping them from want. Southernwood was another plant given to new households because it represented constancy and perserverance. One of southernwood's folk names is Old Man; it represented the man of the house when planted on one side of the door. A rosemary plant on the other side represented the woman of the house. The healthier of the two plants was supposed to indicate which marriage partner had the last say.

A more practical herbal wedding gift would be a bride's box of kitchen herbs. Round, wooden cheese boxes, interesting old boxes or baskets filled with rich soil could hold half a dozen herb plants to grow on an apartment windowsill. Chives, basil, thyme, lemon balm, parsley, and marjoram are useful to any cook as well as insuring love, sympathy, magic and protection from things that go bump in the night. By slipping a few caraway seeds into a husband's pocket, fidelity would be insured. A mullein plant would be nice for brewing up love potions. . . . .

Coddling the Herb Garden

While enjoying your early June herb garden, it is time to think about ways to keep it healthy for the summer.

Seedlings and newly transplanted herbs need plenty of water for a month or so. Established herbs, however, can tolerate very dry weather. Several times a week it is wise to hose the herbs with a brisk spray of fine water to keep the leaves clean. If new plants are set out in the summer, remember to water them deeply and protect them from direct sun for a few days.

Herb gardens usually thrive without very rich soil; however, quick-growing annuals seem to appreciate a little compost or cow manure worked into the soil. In setting out new perennials (like lavender and marjoram), I usually mix one-half cup of compost in the planting hole to give new roots a good start. I never fertilize them again. Some herbs, like mint, will actually develop a rust if the soil is too rich. Some herb garden soil is so poor, however, that stunted growth or poor leaves appear. Liquid manure or a commercial mix of nitrogen-phosphorus-potassium in the ratio of 23-21-17 will give it a mid-summer boost.

Potted herbs do need a little supplement of cow manure from time to time because the soil dries out more quickly and nutrients will drain out with the water. Water potted plants more regularly.

The most threatening insect in the herb garden is an occasional white fly or spider mite. Both of these are easily controlled by a brisk spray of pure water from the hose. NEVER USE INSECTICIDES ON HERBS! Insecticides will leave a residue on herbs that often ruin the delicate and subtle flavor.

Plant diseases in herb gardens are unknown if the garden is kept fairly free of weeds and plants are given fresh air and sunshine. Keep the weeds out of the garden by working at it each day. I take a stroll through the herbs first thing each morning with my cup of tea and pull a dozen or so weeds. I enjoy the cool freshness and never think of it as a chore.

Always mulch the herb garden; it keeps down weeds, holds moisture and makes the garden more pleasing to the eye. Cocoa hulls are the best mulch for these plants. Pine bark mulch is a little too acidic for herbs, although acidic peat moss eventually mixes in for a good herb garden soil.

Appreciate the beauty of your herbs, but do not be timid about cutting and using them. Leave at least a third of the foliage; the plants will love it by growing more handsome and bushy. Make a resolution to use at least one fresh herb each day.

Herbs and Old Roses for Potpourri

Start drying flowers and herbs now for this year's potpourri. Dry everything colorful or aromatic from the garden, and the fields. At this point do not be too selective; color and bulk are the essentials for the potpourri.

June roses are now in full bloom, so search for the sweet-smelling, old-time variety for a particularly rich potpourri. Even the pesky pink Dorothy Perkins rose (the one farmers are always fighting) has a wonderful fragrance when dried. Rose bushes have been known to live hundreds of years, so if you find a rose bush near an old house site, it is sure to be fragrant. Varieties of old roses are known as damask roses, cabbage roses, bourbon roses, or gallica roses. Our modern hybrids and tea roses have been bred for showy flowers, but the rich smell has often been lost along the way.

A rose garden should include several old-fashioned roses just for potpourri. Write for an interesting catalogue from *Roses of Yesterday and Today,* Brown's Valley Road, Watsonville, California. They have hundreds of fragrant old roses from which to choose. I recently ordered the true apothecary rose *(Rosa Gallica `officinalis)* which has been around since the 14th century.

Gather rose petals and other flowers on a clear day just after the dew has evaporated. If the flowers or herbs are wet, it will take them too long to dry and they may mildew. Quick drying retains the color and fragrance for which you are striving. Keep the flowers and herbs out of the sun to dry. Spread petals one layer deep in a shallow basket or on paper; dry them in a dark attic or wooden out-building.

Herbs may also be dried in loose bunches. Secure them with a rubber band which will contract as the stems dry; hang the bunches stem up in the attic or shed.

If the weather is dry, it should only take a week for everything to be chip dry - they should and feel brittle crispy. Store them in an air-tight tin or jar until it is time to mix up the potpourri.

Flowers are the most fragrant when they are just coming

into bloom or are in full bloom. In fact, lavender should only be picked when the buds are the fattest. Fading roses or delphinium flowers with a shriveled look will not be as aromatic or colorful as flowers in their prime. Do not forget to dry a few whole rose buds for the potpourri jar!

These flowers add little fragrance, but dry well and add color to potpourri: delphinium, geranium, statice, bergamot, blue salvia, borage, calendula, marigold, yarrow, feverfew, and larkspur.

These herbs are very fragrant in a potpourri: lavender, rosemary, lemon verbena, lemon balm, the mints, pine needles, sassafras, thyme, woodruff, dried tea leaves, chamomile, penny-royal, sweet marjoram, bay leaves, and basil.

Begin in June and continue all summer to dry potpourri ingredients. Experiment! The winter potpourri jar will echo the summer garden.

"Pleasure is the flower that fades, remembrance the lasting perfume." . . . .Bouffers

Herbal Jellies

The green profusion of the June herb garden will make you ask, "What do I do with all these herbs?" There should be plenty of leaves for drying, using fresh or trying some really fun things. Make herb jelly!

Herb jellies are usually expensive luxury items in the snootiest gourmet grocery, but they can be made simply at home. They turn plain breakfast toast into a delicacy and main dishes or desserts into food for the gods.

I have a basic jelly recipe, but use any favorite jelly recipe.

Linda's Basic Jelly

Combine fruit juice (or water) and the herb in a large kettle; heat to scalding. Take off the heat and let stand for 15 minutes. Strain the liquid through a cloth and return to the kettle with the correct amount of pectin. Stir over high heat until it comes to a full boil. Stir in the sugar or honey and return to the boiling point. Boil two minutes, if you use two ounces of pectin. Remove from heat, skim off foam and pour right away into sterilized jelly glasses. Seal with scalding lids and rings. Turn the jar over to coat the top surface with jelly and turn right side up again to cool.

34

Following are a few combinations that I have tried with success, but be adventurous and try any mixture that sounds good to you.

Thyme Grape Jelly

3 cups grape juice
2 teaspoons dried thyme or 4 teaspoons fresh thyme
2 ounces of pectin
2½ teaspoons lemon juice
3½ cups sugar

Lavender Herb Jelly

3 cups apple cider
1½ tablespoons dried lavender blossoms
2 ounces pectin
4 cups sugar

Place tiny lavender blossoms in the bottom of the jelly glasses before pouring in jelly. Serve with salads and/or desserts.

Marjoram Grapefruit Jelly

¾ cup fresh marjoram or 1 tablespoon dried marjoram
3 cups unsweetened grapefruit juice
1¼ tablespoons lemon juice
2 ounces of pectin
4 cups of sugar

This jelly goes well served with meat.

Mint Lemon Verbena Jelly

1 cup fresh spearmint leaves
1 cup fresh lemon verbena leaves
3 cups apple cider
2 ounces of pectin
4 cups of sugar

This jelly is a real aristocrat of jellies for meat or poultry dishes.

Sage Cider Jelly

3 cups apple cider
2 tablespoons dried sage or ¼ cup fresh sage
2 ounces of pectin
4 cups of sugar

Sage cider jelly spread thinly between a cracker and cheese makes a special snack.

Experiment! I have never tried it, but doesn't strawberry jam flavored with lemon balm sound delicious?

Wild West Virginia Herbs

There is an abundance of colorful wild herbs along country roadsides during these first few weeks of summer. The herbs are there all year, of course, but they are easier for most of us to recognize when they bloom. Queen Anne's lace looks like pineapple weed until the frothy white blossoms appear.

Queen Anne's lace *(Daucus carota)* is a wild carrot brought to America in the 17th century. The fat orange carrot in the vegetable patch will eventually revert to its showier but less tasty roadside cousin if left to seed. At one time this scrawny carrot was cultivated for its medicinal properties. The old herbalists claimed the leaves and seeds were remedies for dropsy, colic and flatulence.

Modern herbalists use the tough Queen Anne's lace root to flavor soups and stews, removing it before the dish is served. Dyers use the white flowers to get a lovely soft green color on wool or linen thread.

White Queen Anne's lace and blue chicory are as much an All-American couple as bacon and eggs. They flower at the same time and grow wild in the same places: dry upland meadows and roadsides. Chicory *(Cichorium intybus)* seed is a favorite food for goldfinch: and the fields of blue and white are often alive with the yellow birds. Herbalists once prescribed crushed chicory leaves as a compress for infections, and the whole plant was used to treat liver and kidney troubles. Chicory roots make a delicious caffein-free coffee. Toast the roots in the oven until they are a rich brown; cool, grind and brew.

Civil War soldiers in this area complained of their bitter chicory coffee, but they were thankful for the hot drink when coffee was impossible to find. Today Southern cooks often flavor soups with a pinch of ground chicory, and the secret of rich New Orleans coffee is the addition of a little chicory.

Mullein *(Verbascum thapsus)* is a dramatic weed with large wooly leaves and a tall spike of yellow blossoms. It thrives in alkaline soil; the Blue Ridge area is rich with mullein. It seems to have been a native both here and in Europe. The first settlers found Indians smoking some leaves and diapering their babies in the largest, softest of the leaves. The Saxons thought a leaf in one's pocket would keep away robbers and wild beasts - all the while making one's thoughts turn to romance. Ancient Romans dipped fresh mullein stalks in melted fat, lighted them and used as torches. Mullein leaves were steeped in oil for use in relieving earaches. Blonde hair was rinsed in a tea made from the flowers. Mighty mullein!

Daisies *(Chrysanthemum leucanthemum)* are escapees from the early settler's gardens. Although the properties are similar to the sweet chamomile, daisy tea is bitter but calming to the nerves. The leaves were once used to bring down a fever. Today's association of daisies with innocence is recent: daisy chains were once worn to attract lovers and repel fleas.

Honeysuckle *(Lonicera caprifolium)* was one of the most useful of wild herbs to our ancestors. A tea from the leaves were gargled for sore throats; the flowers soaked in oil were used to anoint the brow to soothe a headache. Evidently honeysuckle was a pest to early gardeners, too, because Parkinson wrote in 1629, ". . .although it be very sweete, yet I not bring it into my garden but let it rest in his own place. . . ."

Take special notice of these interesting wild things this season. Gather some for their beauty, for the home remedy shelf, or for their fascinating heritage. If they are to be used for seasoning or tea, remember to gather them in an out-of-the-way place and wash well.

June 21 - Festival of Herbs

Summer solstice passes without much more notice than a short comment by the television weather forecaster. In the past it was a celebration of great significance to farming and gardening people - the longest day of the year. The sun begins to drop toward the harvest season and the days become shorter.

To herb gardeners, whose treasured herbs need even more and stronger sun than vegetables or grains, the summer solstice should remain a day to celebrate.

The herb garden itself looks like a festival in late June. Borage blooms the clearest blue imaginable, yarrow is golden or rosy, and lavender and hyssop blossoms give a purple haze. The garden is alive with bees and butterflies. Heady scents of rosemary, chamomile or lemon balm blend and change with the slightest shift of breeze.

Since the feast of St. John the Baptist often fell near the summer solstice, it became known as the Eve of St. John; and the foods and customs blended truth with ancient legend and magic. Great bonfires were lit all over Europe on that night to keep the sun from losing heat. People danced, prayed and repeated almost-forgotten charms to dispel evil and to encourage the long days of sunlight to remain.

Mugwort *(Artemisia vulgaris)* became known as St. John's wort and was made into garlands or chaplets. It was even a legend in England that if you stepped on a mugwort plant after sunset on Midsummer's Eve, a horse would rise out of the ground to carry you until sunrise, leaving you wherever you ended up when the sun peaked through.

Vervaine *(Verbena communis)* bloomed purple in late June and was used with mugworts to make garlands. Larkspur was held up to the bonfires and looked through to insure good eyesight for the coming year.

Use herbs to celebrate midsummer. Make rosemary wine by steeping sprigs of rosemary in a dry white wine for several days before straining, chilling and serving.

Brew up a bowl of punch with borage, the herb of good spirits and happiness.

Borage Punch

Steep a whole stalk of borage (stem, leaves and blossoms) in a gallon dry red wine. Add lemon juice and sugar to taste. Let stand for at least ten hours at room temperature. Chill and serve over ice. Garnish with fresh borage blossoms and slices of lemon.

Make a summer punch with lemon balm *(Melissa officin-alis)*, the herb most loved by bees.

Lemon Balm Punch

Brew up two quarts of a favorite recipe for iced
tea. Add a cupful of crushed lemon balm leaves,
sugar or honey to taste, a twelve ounce can of frozen
undiluted lemonade and a quart of ginger ale or
white wine.

Toss up a giant salad with fresh greens and herbs from your garden. Do not forget lovage leaves, chopped tarragon, chives, salad burnet, parsley and garlic. Try a snip of marjoram.

When your midsummer celebration is over, throw the mugwort, vervaine, or larkspur in the embers (or perhaps the charcoal grill?) and wish for the old magic: "May ill luck depart, burnt up with these."

"Many odde old wives fables are
written of Varvaine tending to witchcraft
and sorcerie, which you may read elsewhere,
for I am not willing to trouble your eares
with reporting such trifles, as honest eares
abhorre to heare."

John Gerard
1633

JULY

High Summer in the Herb Garden

Herbs thrive naturally in the intense heat and sun of high summer, but even healthier plants can be enjoyed if the following suggestions are used.

A second mulching in July is important for several reasons. A two inch layer of mulch keeps the soil moist in dry weather, absorbs more heat than bare earth, and helps to control obnoxious weeds. It is most important to keep the herb garden weed-free as most herbs are small plants which would soon be overshadowed by the troublesome weeds.

An established herb garden will only have to be watered in periods of very dry weather. New plants, seedlings and pots, however, require frequent watering. Water herbs deeply and slowly to encourage tender new roots to grow downward rather than spread out on the surface where they will dry out more quickly. Spray the tops of herbs occasionally to keep them clean and ready for picking. Established rosemary plants need top moisture to stay healthy.

Compost needs to be worked into the soil in areas set aside for gowing annual herbs like dill, basil and borage. The compost should be applied before each new round of crops. Compost or well-rotted manure worked into the soil around new herbs encourages the more desirable slower growth. High nitrogen fertlizers work by encouraging plants to absorb greater quantities of water which produce leafy growth. Herbs are most flavorful when there is less moisture in the leaves. Extra water in the leaves will retard the drying of herbs.

Pull a few weeds each day to stay ahead of the growth. Working in the cool of the early mornings will help sustain the joy of a sweetly fragrant April herb garden.

Cloning Herbs

After an initial investment in a few herb plants, it will seldom be necessary to buy seeds or plants again. Herbs propagate nicely by seed, runners, layering, stem cuttings or root division.

The best time to take cuttings or divisions of herb plants is toward the end of summer when all of us are swamped with the harvest of vegetable and herb garden. Plants seem to be in a determined spurt of growth and cuttings will root quickly. Herbs are seldom interested in sending out new roots when they are winding down the season in early fall.

July is the time to take cuttings of lavender, rosemary, lemon verbena, tarragon, scented geraniums or any other woody-stemmed herbs. Make a cut straight across the stem with a sharp knife below the point at which leaves are attached and where the new stem tips begin to turn woody. Each cutting should be from three to six inches long and have leaves at the tip. Pinch off the larger leaves and immediately insert the cuttings in a box or pot of a moist mixture of sand and vermiculite.

41

It is often suggested that cuttings be kept under plastic or glass for a few weeks, but I have found in the humid Harpers Ferry area that they are healthier and resist rotting if left open in a shady spot and kept well misted and watered. In two weeks the new roots should begin to develop and in four to six weeks they are ready to repot or plant outside.

Some herbs can be easily started by cuttings in water. Mint, lemon balm and pineapple sage make a cheerful row of green when slips are kept in bottles on a windowsill near the kitchen sink. Remember, keep the bottle filled with fresh water.

A few herbs can be successfully increased by seed, but some of the characteristics may not be reproduced. Sage, for example, can be easily grown from seed, but the compact size or variegated color will not recreate in true form.

Chives can be grown from seed, but it is easier to divide the herbs. Some herbs that self-sow readily are savory, hyssop, borage, dill, calendula, caraway, parsley, lemon balm and oregano. A wild array of self-sown seedlings the next year may not be desirable in a very small herb garden. Therefore, collect the seeds as they turn brown and ripe. Store them in tight containers for the winter, and when spring arrives plant them in your selected site.

Viva la Italian Herbs!

With mid-summer comes the abundance of rich Mediterranean vegetables and herbs from the garden. Fat purple eggplants, tomatoes, green peppers and beans are coming on faster than most of us can process them. The natural partner of these vegetables are the tall and bountiful oregano, basil and marjoram. Take advantage of the harvest and use the Italian herbs. Following are some ideas for a delicious blend of herbs and mid-summer vegetables.

Herbal Antipasto

Make an herbal antipasto with almost everything from the garden. Cut green beans, green peppers, zucchini, fennel (stalks sliced like celery). Quarter tomatoes and red Italian onions. Marinate overnight in the refrigerator in a cup of homemade herb vinegar, a little water, olive oil and salt. Serve the antipasto cold on a bed of parsley.

Italian Vinegar

Make a bottle of Italian vinegar to keep on hand for a rich seasoning on summer vegetables and salads. Gather fresh basil, marjoram, oregano, thyme, fennel and leaf of lovage. Or use any herbs you may have on hand. Crush the herbs slightly, pack loosely in a jar, cover with red wine vinegar and add a small, whole garlic clove. Strain the vinegar in a week and use in the vegetable preparations.

Spaghetti Sauce

Try making spaghetti sauce with fresh herbs and tomatoes. If it is too hot for serving pasta, freeze the sauce and serve it on a cool fall evening. Use a favorite recipe for spaghetti, but substitute fresh tomatoes (remove the seeds and skin). Add a sprig of fresh oregano, basil, marjoram and a large handful of freshly chopped parsley. A bay leaf from the garden is the crowning glory. A pinch or two of crushed coriander seed is delicious.

Eggplant

Make an eggplant parmesan with plenty of herbs. Or slice the eggplant in half and broil it. Sprinkle the inside surface with olive oil, a crushed garlic clove and lots of finely chopped basil. Broil slowly for ten to twenty minutes until the eggplant is tender.

Zucchini

Zucchini is always better with Italian herbs. Experiment with oregano, marjoram, and, of course, garlic. Try making zucchini "French fries" by cutting the zucchini into strips and frying. Sprinkle them with parmesan cheese, fresh oregano and salt.

Tomatoes

Tomatoes are inseparable from fresh basil. Never serve a sliced tomato without a sprinkle of freshly chopped basil!

Italian Herbs

Dry basil, oregano, marjoram, thyme and lovage to
crush and store in a jar labeled "Italian Herbs."
Use a pinch to season pizza, lasagne or spaghetti
next winter.

In midsummer, though, use all the fresh Italian herbs
and vegetables and think "Red, White, and Green."

Basil

AUGUST

Flit, Flutter, Buzz, Hmmmm..

Insects intrude upon our lives in August. Chirping crickets invade the house, flies are a nuisance and mosquitoes are biting worse than ever. Our great-grandmothers knew exactly which herbs would repel pesty bugs and make summer life more comfortable. They knew hanging bunches of fresh tansy by windows and doors would discourage flies; and they also knew that dried tansy sprinkled across the ant trail would persuade the little black bugs to find another home.

From June to September my grandmother smelled like oil of citronella as she would rub it on the grandchildren, as well as herself, to ward off chiggers and mosquitoes. It is much more wholesome than commercial insect repellants and I have found it works as well. Oil of citronella, incidentally, is made from lemon balm; and it can still be bought inexpensively from the pharmacy.

The scent of pennyroyal is also effective in keeping biting insects away. Make a strong pennyroyal tea to use as a lotion; or rub a little fresh pennyroyal on your arms and legs when the bugs begin to bite.

Another old time recipe to keep flies outside where they belong is a mixture of cloves, broken bay leaves and dried pennyroyal leaves. Tie the mixture up in little bags and hang them by doorways. The room smells wonderful, but the flies cannot abide it.

A little more exotic formula: wear tonka beans in a little bag around the neck. Patchouli has also been used for centuries as a bug repellant.

Pets will also benefit from a little herbal magic. Sew up a small pillow and stuff it with cedar chips, dried penny-royal and dried chamomile blossoms. Place in the pet's bed and the fleas will find a new home. Dried valerian root, dried rue and even catnip have been sprinkled in dog or cat beds to keep away fleas.

Vanilla bean or dried sweet woodruff have long been used to tuck away in hidden corners of the house for general insect and moth control. They give a wonderful subtle vanilla scent to a room!

Naturalist Hal Borland wrote about the flutter, buzz, click and rattle of insects during their brief span of summer life in a cycle as old as 250 million years. For a long time, too, people have been known to discourage them by using aromatic herbs. It is a good heritage to recall and revive. Keep things simple and keep bugs away without the use of poisons.

If anyone knows of an herb to chase one noisy cricket from under a bed, please let me know - immediately!

Herb Vinegars

This is the time of year for making herb vinegar and almost all fragrant herbs are fair game. The most commonly used vinegars are made of one herb: foliage or seed of dill, caraway mint, tarragon, basil, burnet, or chives. Others are made of combinations of two or more herbs. Experiment with small amounts of several herbs that sound good to you. If your garden is large, revive the old custom of making vinegars from flowers. Rose, violet, carnation, lavender, and elder flower vinegars were very popular during the 19th century.

Herb vinegars are wonderful for salads or deviled eggs - anything in which vinegar is ordinarily used. But herb vinegars also flavor iced drinks, revive low spirits and, when patted on the forehead, will often relieve an aching head.

Herb vinegars are easy to make. To obtain the best flavor, use fresh leaves, flowers, or seeds. When making vinegar from herb foliage, pack a wide-mouthed jar with slightly crushed leaves. Pour cider vinegar to within two inches of the top and cover tightly. Let the mixture stand in a warm dark place for two weeks. Taste the vinegar; and if it is not strong enough, add more herb leaves and infuse another week. Strain the vinegar through several layers of cheesecloth into small bottles; it is now ready to use.

When making herb vinegar from seeds like caraway or fennel, crush several tablespoons of seed for each quart of vinegar and proceed in the same way as for foliage vinegars. Herb vinegar from seeds may have to steep a few weeks longer. A friend of mine insists the vinegar must be hot when poured over the seeds.

To make flower vinegar, collect a cup of petals, add a pint of white vinegar and proceed as usual.

A few herbs, such as basil, tarragon, chives or mint, tend to overpower the others; therefore, be judicious in selection of herbs. Be sure to use chervil, burnet, or marjoram alone since they have very delicate flavors.

Why not try mint vinegar when making cole slaw or french dressing? Burnet vinegar lends a taste of cucumbers to green salad. Try making pickles with basil vinegar instead of the usual dill; and marinate beef or chicken in almost any of the herb vinegars for an unusual flavor.

An Herbal Tea Party

Take the time to brew up a cold, clear and refreshing herb tea; you may never go back to the murky brown drink usually called "iced tea." Herb iced teas are a beautiful crystal green or gold and have all the light taste and aroma of the early morning garden.

Make iced tea the correct way! In so delicate a taste, even the smallest details often make the difference between a mediocre drink and a sublime one. Always use fresh herbs. Tie up the herbs in small cotton bags, rather than a metal tea ball or infuser; and use only a glass or ceramic teapot. Try to use spring water instead of tap water. Never boil herb tea!

My neighbor Bonnie makes a great cup of tea. Slowly measuring the tea and heating water in a delicate old teapot is surely a charming ritual with her..

Bonnie's Herbal Tea

Put in the teapot one teaspoon of dried tea leaves for each cup of boiling water. Use twice the amount of fresh herbs. Add water and steep for ten minutes - no longer or your tea may become bitter.

Some herbs in the garden seem created especially to make the hot weather more tolerable. All of the mint family - peppermint, spearmint, bergamot, and lemon balm are indispensable for cool summer drinks.

Mint Iced Tea

1 cup mint leaves, chopped or crushed
2½ cups boiling water
Sugar or honey to taste

Steep for six minutes

Herb Iced Tea

Make herb iced tea double strength to allow for melting ice cubes. Two generous tablespoons of crushed fresh herb leaves for each glass of iced tea is about the right strength for me.

Tangy Lemon Tea

9 tablespoons thyme
2 tablespoons basil
3 tablespoons lemon balm
2 cups boiling water

Steep almost ten minutes.

Herbal Teas

Lavender and Mint: Combine one part lavender flowers to two parts mint leaves for a tasty and unusual iced tea.

Borage or sweet woodruff: This one claims to restore your droopy heat-laden energy level.

Costmary: It is particularly cooling with a fruity mint taste. Infuse for fifteen minutes, however.

China Tea: Enhance the taste of this one by adding a teaspoon of herb leaves to a regular teapot or cup of tea.

Chamomile: This one has the taste of apples and is refreshing for headaches, upset stomachs, or a chill. Do not drink, however, if you have an allergy to pollen! Peter Rabbit drank it after his bout with Mr. McGregor.

Calendula: Add the dried petals to china tea. It is an aid to beautiful complexion and lightens the spirits.

Catnip: An old time favorite that tastes good, but may make you feel drowsy. It was often used to ward off nightmares and colic.

Lemon Balm: It has a wonderful taste and was once used to relieve feverish colds.

Mints: Everyone likes them! They are said to encourage thinking and intelligence.

Bee Balm: It has a rich fruity flavor and as an American native was enjoyed by the Indians. It grows wild in the Blue Ridge.

Rosemary: A treat with the coolness of a piney forest. The sage-ginger flavor is pleasant. Don't forget rosemary for a good memory.

Sage: To some folks it tastes too medicinal, but it promotes happiness in the home.

Rose Geranium: This is a Victorian favorite. Mix a few leaves and several cloves to your regular China tea.

Try your own blends. I call my favorite "Rocking Chair Tea:" a pinch of orange mint, lemon verbena, rosemary, spearmint, thyme and a few dried lavender flowers.

Most of us know too much caffeine is not healthy, but do not assume that in drinking herb tea it is safe to indulge in unlimited quantities. Herbs are green and growing in your garden, but they do contain tannin and other things with definite soporific or stimulating properties. Enjoy them wisely.

"The Muse's friend, tea does our fancy aid,
Repress those vapours which the head invade,
And keep that palace of the soul serene."

Edmund Waller

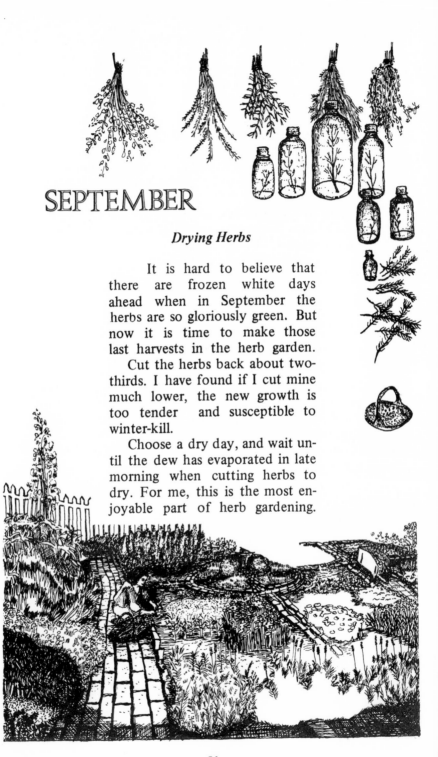

SEPTEMBER

Drying Herbs

It is hard to believe that there are frozen white days ahead when in September the herbs are so gloriously green. But now it is time to make those last harvests in the herb garden.

Cut the herbs back about two-thirds. I have found if I cut mine much lower, the new growth is too tender and susceptible to winter-kill.

Choose a dry day, and wait until the dew has evaporated in late morning when cutting herbs to dry. For me, this is the most enjoyable part of herb gardening.

51

a Christmas potpourri of red and green; or a
pot with lemon balm and dried orange peels;
d some to your bath; or stitch potpourri in a
pillow for transported dreams of sweet-smelling
ens.

Protecting Your Woolens

ly day now, the woolies will come out of storage
of moth balls. We have to either air them for a week
around smelling like the musty inside of a blanket

There is, however, a pleasant way to discourage moths
effectively and with more respect to the nasal senses.
to the garden and the spice shelf!

Many plants in the artemisia family discourage moths
n nibbling. The beautiful gray-foliaged plants take their
ne from Artemis, or Diana, the goddess of the moon. Even
sunny afternoons, artemisias remind me of cool, shimmering
oonlight.

Among them is the elegant French tarragon, *Artemisia
dracunculus,* and the lowly mugwort, *Artemisia vulgaris,* whose
name always makes my children giggle. But most useful as
moth preventatives are wormwood, *A. absinthium,* and *southernwood, A. arbrotanum.*

In fact, in France southernwood is called "garde robe"
and whole sprays of the deeply fringed plant are laid away
with woolens. In England, it is sometimes called "young
lad's love" and boys rub their faces with southernwood ashes
to hurry along a beard.

Wormwood is another artemisia long used to ward off
insect pests. Seventeenth-century herbalist Nicholas Culpepper
has a good word for it: "wormword being laid among cloaths
will make a moth scorn to meddle with cloaths as much as a
lion scorns to meddle with a mouse or an eagle with a fly."

Southernwood and wormwood are hardy, sun-loving
perennials that can be grown for beauty as much as for usefulness. Every old-fashioned garden had southernwood, and it
was often clipped into a hedge. Moths abhor its spicy citrus
scent as much as people like it.

The sweet smells almost make me light-headed when I pile them
into my favorite old basket. An enterprising antique dealer
once labeled it an "herb gathering basket" and I could not pass
it by. My husband insists it was probably used to gather buffalo
chips.

Large-leaved herbs, such as comfrey or sage, dry best
if the leaves are pulled off the stem and spread thinly on screens
or paper.

Dry all herbs in a dark place. Sunlight will bleach them
and leach the precious oils. The attic is one of the best drying
places. A shady kitchen will do fine, also, and it looks and
smells so nice with herbs hanging in it.

Small-leaved herbs, such as thyme or marjoram, dry
well tied in bunches. In fact, if thyme bunches are dried on
a window sill, merely rub the dried herb, and the small leaves
will fall through, leaving bare stems.

Do not throw away the dried stems after stripping the
leaves! Tie them in bundles as small faggots to burn in the
stove or fireplace. They make sweet-smelling kindling and
it is claimed that burning rosemary twigs keeps one young
forever.

As soon as the herbs are crispy dry, store them in glass
jars with screw-on lids. It should take only a few days for
them to dry, but if the weather is damp, put them in a warm
oven for a few minutes.

Any moisture left in the herbs or jars will cause mold.
Once mold appears, throw out the whole batch. It cannot
be redried successfully.

Store jars on dried herbs in a dark cool place. Above
the stove is the wrong place! The heat will dissipate the oils
quickly. Try to keep the leaves as whole as possible and
crumble them with each use. The commercial herbs look pretty
all chopped to a uniform size, but whole, home-grown herbs
will last much longer.

Dried herbs for seasoning and teas are not much good
after a year, so I empty all of last year's into the potpourri
jar.

Chives and parsley are best frozen. Snip them into
¼" pieces, seal them in plastic sandwich bags and stash in the
freezer. When you need chives on the baked potato or parsley
for the soup this winter, take out a handful.

As September comes to a close, your shelf will be lined
with bottles and jars of herbs for the family's pleasure all
winter. It will be your own pharmacy, tea shop and seasoning

rack. Next year why not follow the medieval household tradition of self-sufficiency and establish your own stillroom?

The stillroom was a place set aside to distilll herbal oils, make medicines, liqueurs, jellies and perfumes. Handed down from mother to daughter were the stillroom books with handwritten recipes and formulas. Lady Sedley, an Englishwoman, took pride in her secret cure for aching feet.

Many of the old stillroom manuscripts are still preserved with notations in the margins and marked with X's for particularly good formulas. Handwritings changed and methods evolved, but many of our drugstore necessities came from these old books. Soap is still scented with lavender and furniture polish is still scented with lemon balm.

Did your grandmother use a common toilet water made from rosemary which was sold at most drug stores fifty years ago? It was known as "Hungary Water" and was first made from herbs for the wife of Edward III of England over six hundred years ago.

Make a Potpourri for Winter Fragrance

Enjoy your summer flowers and herbs all winter by capturing their fragrance in a potpourri. Drying blossoms and leaves in combination with other ingredients that will intensify and preserve their fragrance is easy.

In mid-winter when the house is closed up, smelling of soggy wool and stale wood smoke, I open my favorite jar of potpourri and the whole room smells of summer flowers and greens.

Potpourri is actually French for "rot in the pot," referring to the medieval moist jars in which the flowers and herbs actually fermented. Some people still swear by a moist potpourri, but to me it always smells as "rotting in the pot."

Today's commercial trend is toward heavy synthetic fragrance of animal scents like musk. But for more delicate scents, turn to the "rose of our garden and thyme of our fields."

It is not too late to start drying anything colorful left in the garden. Ideally you have already dried roses, lavender, delphinium, larkspur, geranium, calendula and carnations. A few straggly marigolds may be all that is blooming in the September garden, but you can still make a potpourri.

Separate the petal
dry in a dark place for
sheet in a warm o
dry, store them in a

Flower petals
the potpourri. Most
and fixatives.

Dry any herbs gro
planted an herb garden ye
left in the pot after brewing.

After drying flowers a
and oils. Fixatives are essent
adding to the bouquet. Some
sands of years are sandalwood,
root. Orris root is the best with w
violet scent and is easiest to obtain
small chips from a florentine iris roo
macies still carry it.

Essential oils are distilled from
are overpoweringly aromatic. They are ne
a potpourri's fragrance. Good ones to use a
rose, vanilla, clove or lemon. My favorite
bursing the oil is to put a drop on a dried
blossom and crumble it in the potpourri.

Since there are as many preferences as pe
ment with ingredients to obtain just the right com
scents.

Make
citrus
or a
little
gard

An
reeking
or walk
chest.

quite
Look

fro
nar
or
m

Linda's Basic Potpourri

1 quart dried petals and herbs
4 tablespoons orris root
2 drops essential oil

Tumble together. Store in a closed container for a month. Shake the potpourri once a week. When ready, transfer it to a decorative jar and refresh it from time to time with a drop of brandy.

Lavender and rosemary have traditionally been used to discourage moths as well as many other exotic spices that do not grow in our cold weather clime. The May 1864 *Godey's Lady's Book* suggests this recipe:

> "Cloves in coarse powder, one ounce, cassia, one ounce, lavender flowers, one ounce, lemon peel, one ounce. Mix and put them into little bags and place where clothes are kept. They will keep off insects."

To be on the safe side against threatening moths, I combine everything I have heard that works and sew the mixture into little squares to slip between the woolens. We have lots of woolen things in our family and we have never had a moth. It may be the magic of the herbs or the crossing of my fingers, but I will share my mixture with you:

Linda's Moth Mixture

Combine in any amounts whatever of the following you may have: dried southernwood, wormwood, tansy, lavender, rosemary, sweet woodruff, lemon and orange peels, mint, bay leaves, cloves and cedar chips. For the best fragrance, go easy on the tansy and cedar chips.

When you open the blanket chest, I promise you sweet memories of last year and sweet-smelling woolies.

Herb Breads

The Ragos are grateful for the cooler days of September. Busy last-minute harvesting followed by brisk evening air makes our family instinctively hunger for robust autumn food. In the Rago home that means rich homemade bread - herb bread.

Homemade bread from scratch is the best way to enjoy the full flavor of the herbs. Some herbs, such as dill, caraway or anise seeds, will release their flavor through the long moist process of baking bread.

Sesame and poppy seeds have been used for thousands of years to season and garnish breads. Herbalist Pliny described the ancient Greek use of poppy seed. He wrote " . . . country people sprinkle poppy seed on the uppermost crust of their bread, making it adhere by means of the yolk of eggs, the under crust being seasoned with parsley and girth to heighten the flavor of flour."

Garlic Bread and its Variations

Medium sized loaf of French or Italian bread
6 tablespoons of butter
2 cloves of crushed garlic or other herbs such as:

2 teaspoons of dried powdered sage and a pinch of nutmeg (this combination may encourage domestic harmony and ensure partakers of a long life)

or

a pinch of grated onion and 1 teaspoon each of rosemary and thyme (this combination is said to be fine for students as it is claimed to strengthen one's memory)

or

a mixture of marjoram, thyme and summer or winter savory for a flavor very much like pepperoni sausage

Homemade Herb Bread

Use your favorite recipe for white or whole grain bread. Add 1 teaspoon of herbs for each loaf of bread such as:

1 teaspoon caraway seeds
½ teaspoon nutmeg
½ teaspoon rosemary

or

1 teaspoon dill weed or seed

or

1 teaspoon calendula blossoms (this will not add flavor, but will turn white bread a lovely saffron-like color

or

1 teaspoon crushed cumin seeds (adds a special richness to whole grain breads)

Sweet Bread

3 cups white flour
4 teaspoons baking powder
1/3 cup sugar
A pinch of salt
2 eggs
2 cups milk
1½ tablespoons melted butter
3 tablespoons anise seed

Combine the flour, baking powder, salt and sugar. Add eggs, milk, butter and anise seed. Beat well. Bake in two greased loaf pans for ½ hour at 350° F.

Which herbs must be brought in for the winter? Which ones will survive the winter outside? Here in the Blue Ridge, by the end of September it is time to rescue the tender herbs and settle the others in the herb garden for a cold winter. The very tender herbs will blacken at the first frost, so do not waste a minute in bringing in the scented geraniums, lemon verbena, basil and pineapple sage. Early August is the best time to cut from these tender herbs; however, if you have missed the boat, do not give up! Take several stem cuttings, however, to make sure at least one will root.

Rosemary and bay trees will not die with the first frost, but they do need to come in for the winter in the Blue Ridge area. Occasionally rosemary will pull through a mild winter, but it is never worth the risk. Pot the rosemary and bay tree, give them a sunny window, even and cool temperatures and by Christmas you may be rewarded with lovely rosemary flowers.

Basil is nice for a windowsill garden. If outside plants are too bulky, try sowing a pot with basil seed for a tender winter plant. Keep the soil moist and out of the sun until seeds sprout; then give the seedlings plenty of sun and pinch them back to keep bushy plants.

Most other herbs should winter over nicely outside. It is a luxury to have fresh chives, parsley, mint, oregano and borage during the winter, so you may want to pot up a few plants even though their outside siblings are sure to come up again in the spring. Since these herbs only need a temporary home for one winter, cluster them in a strawberry jar for a pretty and convenient inside kitchen garden. A round wooden cheese box filled with good soil and a medley of herbs makes a beautiful garden for a windowsill.

Try a winter tea garden of lemon verbena, lemon balm, thyme, sage, sweet marjoram and mint. These plants are grown more closely together than usual, so fertilize them regularly and use often to keep them bushy and small.

There are a few things to remember to keep these outdoor herbs happy inside. Keep them cool (50°to 70°F); make sure they have good drainage - clay pots are best; give them plenty of sunlight (without enough natural light, try flourescent lighting of 14 hours a day at 16 inches above the herb); keep them away from direct heat or blasts of cold air; and check regularly for insects. Brisk rinsing under the tap each week should keep foliage clear of bugs.

Inside herbs reward you with fine flavors, scents and good health. A lingering ghost of the luxuriant herb garden in summer will sit on your windowsill until another growing season begins.

OCTOBER

Herbs for "Filthy Flimie Humors"

The herb garden has turned the corner from summer's frenetic growing to fall's inactivity. Calendula stalks are brown, yarrow looks ragged and borage is turning hoary and coarse. But to me there is something abidingly noble about an herb garden after its lush green has faded.

To understand the heritage of herbs, an examination of an earlier metaphysical assumption totally different from our own is necessary. Most of our herb lore comes from a time in the late medieval world when it was assumed everything in the universe was created for the dual purpose of God's glory and human welfare.

This philosophy was the seed-bed for the great herbalists of the sixteenth through eighteenth centuries like William Turner and John Gerard. I love to spend a winter evening chuckling over facsimiles of their works. Gerard claims that fleabane does indeed ". . .purgeth the head mightily of foul and filthy flimie humors." Have you suffered from filthy flimie humors lately?

We should not, however, dismiss these herbalists as entirely ignorant. They stimulate our imagination to understand how our forefathers were trying to establish a relationship between themselves and the universe.

Sometimes they did branch off into pure folly as with the Doctrine of Signatures in which plants were seen as clues from God; or liverwort cured the liver because the leaf was liver-shaped; or walnuts cured headaches because the kernel looked like a brain.

Herbalists, however, also gave birth to the sciences of medicine and pharmacology, as well as horticulture and systematic botany.

Remember, not only harmless folk cures come from herbs, but also powerful medicines, such as oleander-derived tranquilizers. From foxglove comes the heart medicine digitalis. Willow leaves have been used for hundreds of years to treat arthritis and rheumatism; and it is now known willow contains salicylic acid, which is used in making aspirin.

I am convinced that most folk cures, however, work primarily on the power of positive thinking. A young woman recently related to me that drinking clary sage tea had improved her eyesight. I was a little surprised because traditionally clary sage was used on the eyes externally. The water-soaked seeds formed a soothing gelatinous mass which was used to clean irritants from the eye. The woman's eyesight may seem better, but I cannot wonder what clary sage tea is doing to her innards. It is foolish to treat yourself with herbs unless you have undertaken some extensive research.

Not only did our ancestors view their relationship with plants differently, they used and valued them differently. Today's gardening trend of merely growing vegetables for food and flowers for pretty color seems to omit so much from the total picture. Herbs were complete identities with which to be lived - having their own subtle fragrances and powers. Did you know there were herbal salves to anoint the brow against "elf or goblin night visitors?"

Corn Dollies Bring Good Luck

October weekends bring harvest fairs of some sort to the country towns. The last of the long rows of corn are cut and stored, apple boxes are full, and the harvest of the final straggle of vegetables before black frost is in progress. The last herbs are gathered and hung, and there is just enough basil left for one more batch of vinegar.

It is time to celebrate the harvest - with herbs of course! The rich symbolism of herbs is perfect for expressing our harvest feelings. A bowl of potpourri is the culmination of an entire herb summer, a colorful herb wreath hanging in the kitchen symbolizes the cycles of the seasons, and an herb-lady doll hanging in the parlor symbolizes fertility for the coming year.

Why not make an herb doll for your home? Traditionally herb dolls were made with straw or corn husks. Corn husk dolls may have first been made by our Appalachian forebears who remembered the "Corn Dollies" made in rural England. (Corn in England and Europe referred to all grains with heads such as wheat or rye. Maize was the name for our corn.)

These harvest dolls were fashioned from the last stalks of corn to be cut and were decked with herbs and flowers. Since the feast of St. Michael fell at the end of September, michaelmas daisies were often included. Chamber's *Book of Days* tells of the harvest doll in old England: "It was brought home from the field in triumph with music of fiddles and bagpipes. It was set up conspicuously that night at supper and was usually preserved in the farm's parlor for the remainder of the year."

These harvest ladies had various names and forms in different areas. They were called Countryman's Favor, Earth Mother, Corn Baby, Ivy Girl, Welsh Border Fan and many other names.

In our home the harvest doll is made by Grandmother Vera Rago with long strands of straw or raffia tied over a small ball for the head while the remainder of the straw hangs loosely for the body. Button eyes are sewn on. Arms are tied through the body, a calico sunbonnet and apron are added, and a tiny basket of herbs placed on her arm. She presides over our harvest home with sprigs of lavender for purity, rosemary for remembrance, bay for triumph, tansy for immortality, sage for domestic happiness and thyme to help us keep our minds open enough to see the fairies dance.

Halloween Herbs

Herbs have always been used to protect country folk from the witches, goblins and other mysterious spirits released to the skies on Halloween. Our cheerful Halloween celebrations with bright pumpkins, mulled cider and chubby trick-or-treaters in bunny suits are faint recollections from a remote past.

Roman and Greek harvest customs have combined with the ancient Druid festival of Samhain, when the souls of all the wicked dead were allowed to roam the countryside for one night - our Halloween. It was a time of magnificence, yet terror, to our ancestors; and they looked to the power of their herbs to protect them.

Centuries ago on the day before Halloween the farm family would be busy hanging osier twigs or mountain ash berries at all the doors and windows. Barns and pig sties were included - for no witch would dare cross a protected threshhold. A very hot oak fire was kept burning on the hearth to discourage errant spirits from coming down the chimney.

Rue and dill are traditional witch repellants; and honesty (or the money plant) with its round silver discs is avoided by evil spirits who fear light and seek darkness. Pennyroyal, chervil and artemisia discourage evil; witches are said to always avoid yellow flowers since these represent the sun and goodness. Wear an angelica leaf on Halloween for portable protection.

Use the herbs of your garden in celebrating Halloween. In our family the rich colors and fascinating symbolism add spice to this fun folk festival. Make an autumn Halloween swag for the door with a base of silvery artemisia. Tuck in a few orange rowan berries or bittersweet. Add some yellow chrysanthemums or marigolds as special protection. Include honesty, deep red oak leaves. Tie the whole swag with a clear toned bell that rings when the door opens. Your door will say a cheerful "Welcome" to friends and a definite "Keep Out" to any local witches.

Have a wonderful Halloween and remember,
> "Trefoil, vervain, John's wort, dill
> Hinders witches of their will."

—Guy Mannering

64

NOVEMBER

Preparing Herbs for Winter

It is now time to put the herb garden to bed for the winter. The first frosts have blackened the tender herbs, and even the more hardy ones are scraggly and weather-beaten. November almost always provides a few days of Indian summer and a good excuse to work amid the plants.

one last time before winter. If neatness is of prime importance to you, trim everything back to an inch or so off the ground and add the clippings to the compost pile. If, however, the survival of healthy herb plants through the winter is more important to you, let the brittle tops stand in the garden.

The stalks collect blowing leaves and snow for a blanket against icy winds which are so damaging to perennial plants. Winter birds love the unkempt herb garden; it is a cozy place to escape the winter winds and a convenient launching pad to the bird feeder. Birds are always important to a garden for keeping out unwanted bugs next summer.

Because herb gardens are not apt to harbor plant diseases the danger of wintering-over infected foliage is almost non-existant. In fact, organic vegetable gardeners often use herb cuttings as part of a winter mulch to discourage pests.

November is a good time, though, to pull out the remains of any leftover weeds, and to add manure or compost to the areas that will be planted next spring with fast growing annuals. Sprinkle a little lime around the lavender and put a large stone on the windward side for protection.

Enjoy the herb garden in these shorter days of bright sunlight. The rich autumn scents of wood smoke and the dying foliage combine in the herb garden with the pungency of sage and thyme. It is very different from the sweet smells of the summer herb garden. It is full of the magic and poignancy of approaching winter. Savor the deep brown of old oregano blossoms and the black-green of germander and thyme. The soft greys of lavender, sage and santolina are often most beautiful in the autumn herb garden.

When the hard winter sets in after Christmas, there will be time for serious mulching; and when spring arrives, it is time for tidying up the herb garden, but for now, let it rest.

"The knot and the border, and the rosemary gay
Do crave the like succour, for the dying away..."
— *Thomas Tusser, 1573*

Making a Fragrant Herb Wreath

In the first days of November the roadside, as well as the garden, is abundant with material for making a fragrant herb wreath.

Sweet wormwood *(Artemisia annua),* often called myrrh locally, has formed brown-green spires along fence rows. Symmetrical brown seed stalks of perilla (known as wild basil here in the Blue Ridge) are plentiful. Gather armfuls for a wreath.

Wreath making is a noble and ancient practice, and the circle has long been symbolic of immortality. To me, a harvest herb wreath particularly brings to mind the cycle of our growing season and the celebration of its fruitfulness.

The rich natural colors and light fragrance of a herb wreath give the senses pleasure. The symbolism of the plants enrich our spirit. Include bay leaves for triumph, rosemary for remembrance, lavender for purity, tansy and yarrow for everlasting life and rue to discourage evil. Add southernwood to encourage romantic love and sage to promote domestic tranquility.

I start my herb wreath with a ten inch straw base. Sweet wormwood or the artemisia Silver King make good background material, but use anything that dries well and is plentiful in the garden. To make a strong wreath that will last many years, I wrap florist wire around several full three-inch stems and anchor the wire ends into the straw. Hold the wreath up often to be sure it remains symmetrical. Once a full base is complete, the real fun of making a wreath begins. Adorn the wreath with sprigs of any herb having a pleasant fragrance. Stay away from chives and garlic.

If the stems are sturdy like thyme or rosemary, just punch them into the base. If the herb is more fragile, like rue, or has a heavy flower head like yarrow, wrap the stem with florist wire.

For my kitchen wreath, I wire on several cinnamon sticks, a tiny circle of cardamon pods and several bay leaves. Rust or golden bows of gros-grain ribbon add to the visual effect.

A very Victorian herb wreath can be made by adding dried rosebuds and lavender or using old lace for a bow. For Christmas add holly or boxwood and tuck in new clippings of fresh herbs all winter.

Hang the herb wreath where it can be enjoyed every day. Let it be a reminder that the green herb garden is coming full circle and only temporarily resting until spring.

Herb Pillows

Herb-filled pillows are pure luxury from the herb garden. Dry sweet-smelling herbs and fill small pillows to toss on the bed or a favorite chair for snoozing. Our ancestors often tied scented pillows to the "wings" of wingback chairs.

Herb pillows have a long tradition. In Biblical times, mothers filled pillows with mandrake root to protect children from evil spirits. During medieval days the pleasant smells of herbs were assigned special healing effects on the spirit as well as the body. Lemon balm would disspell nightmares and rosemary would cure insomnia. In 1653 an herbalist wrote, "Sweet perfumes work immediately upon the spirits, for their refreshing; sweet and healthful ayres are special preservatives to health and therefore much to be prised."

Although we do not believe in such quick cures for a sick mind or spirit anymore, we do know the stimulating effect of smells. Who doubts the jarring whiff of smelling salts or the soothing of tense nerves with a quiet fragrance? Our sense of smell is the only one we cannot shut off! We can close our eyes to beauty, plug our ears and refuse to taste or feel the good things of life, but as long as we breathe, we cannot refuse to smell.

Create a mint-filled pillow to encourage mental alertness and to impart wisdom. Gather as much mint as necessary to dry and stuff a four by six inch pillow. Add a little dried lavender, thyme, rosemary and a drop or two of lavender oil. This pillow makes a great gift for a student. Placed on the sofa, it will insure brilliant conversation when company arrives.

Fill a snooze pillow with dried rosemary, costmary, rose petals and thyme. Add a teaspoon of orris root for a fixative. This pillow will lull you into a deep sleep as surely as the soothing strains of a lullaby.

For soothing a headache, mix several types of dried mint, bee balm and a teaspoon of orris root to fill the pillow. The scents of camphor in the bee balm and menthol in the mint are invigorating.

Sleeping with a tiny pillow of dried lemon balm is said to keep bad dreams away: and pillows filled with dried hops are reputed to make nights more comfortable for those with stuffy noses. The smell of dill is thought to induce sleep; often small pillows stuffed with dill seed were put in the baby's cradle.

Make your own herb pillow with your favorite herb scents. Sweet dreams!

DECEMBER

An Old-Time Herbal Christmas

Decorating for the holidays begins the first week of December at our house. It is Old Time Christmas in Harpers Ferry! Townspeople dress for the 19th century festivities in period clothing, homes are lit, and fresh greens are everywhere. Herbs, too, express the joy and celebration of Christmas!

The first decoration, to prepare is the herb wreath or garlands to welcome friends at the door. Sprigs of herbs are tucked in among the fresh lemons and apples tied to boxwood wreaths.

Thyme is used because its blue flowers are the color of Mary's robe, bay leaves for the nobility of the Christ child, lady's bedstraw because it filled the manger, and, of course, rosemary, the herb whose piney scent is most associated with Christmas and remembrance. Some years, just to be safe, I stick in a twig of rue to discourage the scrooges.

Our children begin to get impatient to cut the Christmas tree. We never have a symmetrical *Good Housekeeping* tree, but it is always beautiful with echoes of good times and herb traditions. We cut a red cedar which Grandpa Ours is always glad to get out of the orchard or pasture. The tall thick upward reaching tree usually comes already decorated with blue berries. In the 19th and early 20th centuries before Christmas trees were transported long distances, these home-grown cedars were the most usual Christmas trees here in the Blue Ridge.

Dignified cedars and junipers have long been venerated herbal trees. Ancient Greeks burned their berries to keep away the furies. In Italy stables were protected from thunderbolts by juniper. Cedar was strewn on Scandinavian floors as an antiseptic and burning branches were said to drive away "aire which bringeth plague." In England a cedar is often seen growing beside the door because of its reputation for driving away witches who were bound by black law to count every needle before entering. If the witch lost count, she had to start over and would finally give up and go away in frustration

Kissing balls are another holiday tradition entwined with herb lore. Holly, boxwood and mistletoe are the well-known traditional materials for kissing balls; however, thyme, santolina and rosemary are often included. The rich fragrance makes everyone happier, and rosemary will insure a memorable kiss.

To make a kissing ball, start with a raw potato. Make holes in the potato with a tooth pick every inch or so and insert the stem of boxwood, rosemary or any evergreen. When the kissing ball is fat and full, tie it up with a red ribbon and a brass bell to hang above a much-used doorway. The kissing ball will stay fresh for several weeks.

Be aware of all the herbs and spices lending scents, tastes and beauty to the season. Frankincense and myrrh were herbal gifts worthy of the Christ child. Would it be Christmas without nutmeg and cinnamon?

Follow the 17th century instruction to bring in the wassail " . . .bearing a brown bowl drest with ribands and Rosemary . . ."

70

Pomanders for the Holidays

The wonderful aroma of a bowl piled high with pomanders is as much a part of the holiday season at our house as the smell of roasting turkey. The rich combination of oranges and cloves cured in spices makes rooms, closets or drawers fragrant.

During the Middle Ages, nobles wore rich jeweled pendants especially made to hold exotic herbs and spices whose fragrant oils were thought to ward off disease. These were early pomanders. Sometimes crushed herbs were tightly compacted into a paste ball; or beeswax was used as a medium.

Doctors always carried them to ward off odors. Lawyers and judges in closed courtrooms with prisoners suffering from jail fever considered their pomanders essential. Strollers along streets with open sewers often sniffed at sweet herbs in the hollow heads of canes.

By the time our ancestors were colonizing America, however, oranges studded with cloves were used as pomanders by almost every household prosperous enough to buy them. Soon it was discovered that our native apples worked almost as well.

To make a pomander, choose firm thin-skinned apples, oranges, lemons, limes or grapefruit. Stud the fruit with whole cloves not more than a quarter inch apart. Cloves placed too tightly may split the fruit.

When the pomander is completely studded, roll it well in the spice mixture of equal parts cinnamon and powdered orris root. Nutmeg, allspice and ginger may also be added. The mixture is the secret to successful pomanders. The spices prevent mold; the orris root is a fixative which will prolong the fragrance almost indefinitely.

Place the pomander in a dry, warm place for several weeks to dry. The pilot light in a gas oven is a perfect spot.

The pomander may be tied with a ribbon to hang over a coat hanger (gives the coat a wonderful fresh scent), or tied up in a cloth to place in a drawer or chest. Pile several pomanders in a bowl for a delightful way to sweeten a room.

When the pomander becomes dusty or loses some aroma, rinse it off under the tap quickly, put it in the oven on the lowest setting for ten minutes and it will be like new again. Some of my pomanders are over ten years old.

Make a pomander early in December and it will be dry and ready to give as a thoughtful Christmas present by December 25. It makes a noble gift, also. Queen Elizabeth I received from a gallant courtier "a gyrdle of pomanders," the traditional gift for "fayre ladies" at Christmas.

A COMPENDIUM OF FAVORITE HERBS

'every plant must bear its part, and they must fall into their places like the notes in music!'

—John Evelyn, 1664

Bay Leaves: Emblems of the Sun God

Laurus nobilis

Bay has been paired with rosemary for an eternity by the herbalists. Garlands of bay leaves worn by heroes were interlaced with rosemary even before the heyday of Rome. My tall bay tree must feel comfortable wintering beside grande dame rosemary.

A large bay is a magnificent evergreen plant and is nearly priceless. In its native Mediterranean region, the bay *(Laurus nobilis)* often grows to be a 60-foot tree. In the Blue Ridge climate, however, the best way to grow a bay tree is in a tub. I haul mine out in May and bring it inside in early October.

By keeping the large, shiny green leaves pruned from the main stem, my bay has begun to look like a little tree. It is slowly growing, but the best I can hope for is that it will eventually reach 10 feet.

I have never been able to root a bay cutting, although it is the traditional way to propagate. Patience is a key ingredient, I am sure, because it can take up to six months for a cutting to root. A reliable nursery is the best bet for a baby bay tree. However, expect to pay several dollars for one.

The leaves can be picked and used year-round. Frequent users of the dried bay leaves will find a pleasant surprise when using the fresh green ones.

The fragrant bay leaf can be used with soups, stews, meat, fish, pudding, pickles, cakes and an almost endless list of foods.

Placed in cannisters, bay leaves keep bugs from flour and cereals. In the Middle Ages, *The Goodman of Paris* states that sweet smelling bay leaves were "layde amonge clothes."

Bay leaves were often steeped in water used to wash hands and faces. In fact, *Grete Herball* says bay water is good "against a manner of red things that come in young folks' faces." Gerard's herbal declares "common drunkards were accustomed to eat in the morning, fasting two (bay) leaves thereof against drunkeness."

Unfortunately our native laurels are all very poisonous. If you cannot be sure it is *Laurus nobilis,* do not use it.

Man has long held a superstitious regard for the beautiful bay. The Greeks dedicated it to Apollo and viewed it as an emblem of the sun god's powers. Shakespeare in *Richard II* warns the audience that things are really bad because "the bay trees in our country are all withered."

An old herbal claims one is safe from devils, witches, thunder and lightning in a place where a bay tree grows. It never hurts to have a bay tree around, especially on Halloween.

Basil: the Queen of High Summer

Ocymum basilicum

Fresh and green in the heat of mid-August stands basil, the symbol of high summer. At this time of year, it is almost a yard high and almost ready to burst into bloom. It seduces every insect with its heady, spicy scent. It is the "hussy" of the herb garden. There is nothing subtle about basil, and once you have used it fresh, you will be addicted.

Fat, red tomatoes are basil's natural counterpart finely chopped and sprinkled fresh over juicy slices. Eggs, cheese, liver and mushrooms are also transformed by highly pungent, shredded basil leaves.

Remember, use basil alone and have a light hand, at first. It disdains sharing the spotlight and will overpower most other herb flavors. A small pinch goes a long way. Also, remember to use one half as much dried basil as fresh. Refer to pages 42 - 44 for recipes using basil.

Ocymum basilicum is the botanical name for sweet basil. *Ocymum minimum* is bush basil. Both are flavorful, but the bush basil only grows a foot tall. Very pretty, purple basils are advertised in the seed catalogs as having the traditional basil flavor, but to me they taste more clove-like.

All basils are annuals. They should be planted when the ground is thoroughly warmed. When tomato plants are set out, it is a good time to sow basil seed. Since basil plants are fast-growing, fleshy plants, the soil should be richer than for most herbs. The vegetable garden is a good place for a few basil plants. Keep the flower spikes pinched off and the plants will be bushier.

Everyone has a pet way to keep basil through the winter. Some of my friends swear by freezing it; some quick dry it in the oven; and others pack the leaves between layers of coarse salt. I prefer old-fashioned air drying. The flavor is stronger, and I do not mind the darker color that is avoided by freezing. It may be that I have an affinity for the easiest way.

Cut the largest stalks with the most leaves in late morning on a sunny day. Tie three or four stalks together with a rubber band, that will contract when the moisture evaporates. If string is used, the bunches will sometimes fall apart.

Hang the bunches in a dry spot away from sunlight. Hang basil in the kitchen, and there is an added bonus of its wonderful aroma.

Basil's glory is ephemeral. With the first light frost, basil will wilt and blacken. For a few pots of fresh basil in a sunny window this winter, sow the seeds in August. The garden plants will probably be too large to pot up for winter.

In India, basil is a sacred plant. Dioscorides, a 6th century Greek herb writer, cautions that eating too much "dulls the eyesight." Young Italian boys give basil leaves as symbols of love, and the 16th century English herbalist Tusser wrote of basil "it receives fresh life from being touched by a fair lady." All of us will receive a freshness by a touch of basil.

Beebalm: An American Native

Beebalm is one of the few native American herbs, a fascinating plant from an historical point of view and a richly fragrant one. The blossoms are the showiest in the herb garden. No traditional herb garden or flower bed should be without beebalm.

As an American perennial, it was an important source of tea in the colonies after the Boston Tea Party. Indians were using beebalm as a stimulant and to soothe sore throats and colds. Apparently they shared this remedy with settlers very early because it is recorded that John Bartram of Philadelphia mailed seeds to England in the 1740's. It is still grown and highly prized in England and Europe.

Because the fragrance and taste of beebalm is very much like the fruit of the tropical bergamot orange tree, the herb is sometimes called bergamot, particularly in Europe. From the Indians we get the name Oswego Tea. It still grows wild in profusion around Oswego, New York, where it was once cultivated and sold by the Oswego Shaker settlement.

Prolific beebalm grows several feet tall in one season and produces an abundance of large leaves. The foliage has a wonderfully rich fruit-like taste when brewed into tea. Even those who have not acquired a taste for herb tea will like a beebalm leaf in china tea. Try flavoring apple jelly or fruit drinks with beebalm.

In the Blue Ridge, beebalm grows wild in cleared parts of the forest such as old wood roads or in unused pastures. This herb, *Monarda fistulosa,* has large fuzzy lavender flowers growing on a very erect square stalk. It can easily be transplanted to the garden by digging up a clump of the shallow roots in spring or fall and replanting them in a moist soil with sun or partial shade. Beebalm will become a decorative mainstay of the herb garden, blooming from July to September.

Occasionally, along streams or in shaded marshy places, the bright scarlet beebalm *(Monarda didyma)* can be seen growing. It is more common in New England where country people call it red bergamot or scarlet monarda. Most nurseries carry the red beebalm, if you are unable to find a wild clump. One called Mahogany is particularly colorful and hardy. The Croftway Pink is a lovely salmon pink. To attract hummingbirds, grow red beebalm.

The entire plant is fragrant with the leaves and flowers used in potpourri or bath herbs. They can be used fresh in summer and then dried for use next winter. Even the dried stems (after the leaves are stripped) make a sweet smelling kindling in the fireplace.

Keep beebalm bushy by harvesting it two or three times a season. After the first blooming, cut the stalks back to about three inches. The foliage tends to get straggly, anyway, if it is allowed to grow all summer. When it is cut back, beebalm will bloom several times a summer.

Introduce beebalm into your garden, cherish its patriotic heritage and be cheered by its sparkling color.

Borage: The Courage Giver

Borago officinalis

"I Borage, Give Courage . . ." is the ancient Greek saying which launched borage's *(Borago officinalis)* reputation for bringing courage and dispelling melancholy. It is still the most cheerful plant in the herb garden. Blue star-shaped flowers bounce in the wind all summer.

Borage is a hardy annual. Plants grown from seed in spring will re-seed for years. Three generations of the plant will often grow in one season. Instead of keeping the borage pinched back, I usually let it rise high in the garden, pull out the straggly plants in July or August and let the tender self-seeded plants take over. I do the same thing in September.

Mature plants will grow almost three feet tall, but the branches droop prettily and the plant often takes up several square feet. Since the striking blue star flowers with black centers look best from below, borage would be beautiful growing on a bank or wall. Experiment with borage in hanging baskets.

The tender young leaves give a cool cucumber flavor to salads; the more mature leaves are pleasant tasting "greens." Borage has a hairy texture which some herb scholars insist is responsible for the derivation of its name from the low Latin term for flock of wool: *Burra.*

Today, as in the past, the prime use of borage is in making and flavoring drinks. Ancient warriors drank wine steeped in borage to give them courage in battle. Why not garnish the cocktail with a sprig of borage or float several of its flowers in the lemonade? Any cool summer drink will taste better with the addition of a crushed borage leaf. The leaves can be dried for a winter tea. Make sure the leaves are dried throughly and stored in an airtight container because they will draw dampness and mold easily.

Fresh borage on the windowsill all winter is easy to grow and may be what you need to ". . .exhilarate the spirits and drive away dusky melancholy." Remember, give inside borage the same requirements as outside: dry, light soil and plenty of sunshine.

Bee Bread is another common name for borage. It relies completely on bees for pollination, and the cluster of blue flowers are almost always surrounded with bees. It yields an excellent honey, and is often grown for that purpose.

Borage has traditionally been grown among strawberry plants, and they are said to enrich and protect one another from insects and disease. However, the borage must be kept pinched back or there will be all borage and few strawberries.

Medieval ladies embroidered borage flowers on almost every piece of needlework; the curling tendrils with blue stars are often included in modern needle and fabric design. The symbolism is long forgotten, but the little flower is part of our heritage.

Truly worthy of its Welsh name "Herb of Gladness," it has been said a garden without borage is like a heart without courage.

Bacon's Burnet

Poterium sanguisorba

Salad burnet *(Poterium sanguisorba)*, a perennial herb, will not be large enough to provide a steady supply of leaves until the second year of growth.

A few burnet leaves give the cool taste of cucumber to a salad. Chopped burnet in creamed cheese or butter flavors them in an unusual and delicious way. Fresh burnet steeped in wine vinegar for several weeks makes a salad vinegar with the taste of cucumbers. Summer drinks with a burnet garnish are refreshing.

Burnet does not dry well, and it is almost impossible to transplant burnet or keep the plant healthy indoors for the winter. Fortunately, salad burnet often keeps a few green leaves all winter in the Blue Ridge area.

In England burnet was used as a forage plant because it would grow and keep green all winter in dry barren pastures, feeding sheep when grasses were scarce. It still thrives on poor, well-drained alkaline soil. The pilgrims brought burnet to Massachusetts as a year-round source of fresh greens for themselves as well as livestock. Burnet tea was thought to control hemorrhaging and to have astringent properties.

Burnet has " . . .two little leaves like unto the winges of birdes, standing out as the bird setteth her wings out when she intendeth to fly . . ." writes herbalist Turner in 1568. The leaves resemble small rose leaves and do grow out from the stem like wings. It is a pretty little plant with flowers of a deep brownish red growing on round heads. Most of the year the leaves lie flat, almost on the ground, but they rise up like a fountain when the plant blooms. Keep the blossoms pinched off unless you want it to self-seed.

Sir Francis Bacon suggested it be planted in alleys to "perfume the air most delightfully being trodden upon and crushed." For me, burnet evokes scenes of Elizabethan England in my little herb garden. It is an herb which was known and used by almost everyone in Shakespeare's day, but which has underservedly gone out of fashion.

> "The even mead, that erst brought
> sweetly forth
> The freckled Cowslip, Burnet
> and green Clover."
>
> Henry V., V. ii. 48

Nepeta cataria

Catnip Fever

Mouse is the dignified black and white cat next door. She is getting on in years and usually stays disdainfully aloof from the neighborhood commotion of children and dogs, so it always starts my day with a chuckle when I see her stride to my catnip patch and make an old fool of herself. She nibbles the leaves and purrs. Then she rolls in the catnip and jumps like a kitten in frenzied ecstasy.

Catnip *(Nepeta cataria)* has always been mysterious to people because of its strange allure to felines. In almost every language the name includes the word "cat:" In French it is *Herbe aux Chats;* in German it is *Katzenminze;* and in Italian it is *Erba gatta.* From kittens to lions, all cats love it. It is the oil exuded from a bruised or dying plant that drives them wild Hence comes the old folk saying "If you set it, the cats will

80

eat it, If you sow it, the cats won't know it." Most of us in this part of the country do not have to sow it since catnip has naturalized and spread profusely.

Find a spot to gather the wild catnip, or mark the plant and go back in early fall to dig up several roots to plant in the herb garden. Catnip has sturdy square stems like other members of the mint family. It is set with two or three heart-shaped leaves of a soft frosty green. The leaves are roundly serrated and have a coat of soft down. By August catnip is blooming with pale purple-like flowers in dense clusters on spikes. Decorative strains have been developed with very beautiful clear blue flowers. They are listed in nursery catalogues as *Nepeta macrantha.*

Cut and dry the herb for tea and the pleasure of your cat. Cut two thirds of the plant, including flowers, stems and leaves. Hang in loose bunches in a hot, dry and dark place for a few days. Then crumble the leaves and flowers into bottles and jars or stitch up the dried herb in little cloth bags for the cat to sniff and bat.

Catnip tea is soothing to an upset digestive tract and will often make the drinker drowsy. It is one of the few remaining herbal remedies still passed down among country people. Ask any Appalachian woman what to do for the baby's colic and she will surely suggest catnip tea (or maybe "nep tea" as it is sometimes called).

Brew catnip tea as with any other herb tea. Use one teaspoon of dried catnip or twice the amount of fresh catnip for each cup of tea. It is good hot or cold and lemon makes a good addition.

Tough Chamomile Triumphs

Chamomile blossoms look like cheerful little daisies. Chamomile *(Anthemis nobilis)* is one of the few herbs whose flowers are the most useful part. Children seem to naturally love the little feathery plant; our daughter Jane is very proud of her task as family harvester of chamomile. Remember when Peter Rabbit was given a stiff dose of chamomile tea after his famous bout with Mr. MacGregor?

Anthemis nobilis

81

There is also an annual chamomile *(Matricaria chamo-milla)*, sometimes called German chamomile, with coarser foliage but the same flavorful characteristics. It is the creeping perennial Roman chamomile, however, that I grow for its bountiful harvest. It seems to thrive on neglect here in the Blue Ridge.

Sow chamomile seed outdoors on a sunny May day in moist, well-drained soil. It likes sun but will tolerate a little shade. In the misty, mild climate of England whole chamomile lawns were grown, but our seasons are too rugged to rely on chamomile groundcovers.

Our native feverfew *(Pyrethrum parthenium)* is closely related and sometimes called wild chamomile, but it lacks the distinctive apple-like scent and properties of the true chamomile.

In fact the apple scent and taste is so pronounced it has earned the plant's name from the Greek "kamai" (on the ground) and "melon" (apple). The Spanish name is Manzanilla (little apples).

The flowers are ready to harvest when the white petals around the center disc curl back and the yellow center stands up. Use them fresh or spread them out thinly in a shallow basket to dry in a warm, shady spot. Next, store in an airtight container. Even those who only tolerate most herb teas often enjoy chamomile tea because of its rich apple flavor. One friend, unfortunately, who was given chamomile as a child for upset stomachs, says the taste of chamomile only reminds her of the stomach aches.

Two teaspoons of fresh chamomile or one teaspoon of dried chamomile will make one cup of tea. Steep it in hot water for five to ten minutes as with any herb tea. A little honey particularly enhances chamomile tea, and it is delicious as iced tea. It was used traditionally to soothe mild indigestion, calm the nerves, drive away fevers and prevent nightmares. A weaker tea makes a refreshing skin lotion and blonde hair is said to be sunnier when rinsed with chamomile tea.

The ancient Egyptians dedicated chamomile to the sun; in Europe during the Middle Ages it was dedicated to St. Anne, mother of the Virgin Mary. It was a favorite flower for making medieval garlands. In Elizabethan England it was a popular groundcover for walks or banks to sit on. Shakespeare's Falstaff sternly reminds us "Though Camomile the more it is trodden on the faster it grows, yet youth the most it is wasted the sooner it wears." Henry IV, Pt. I, II, iv.

Chervil - The Parsley of Gourmets

Anthriscus cerefolium

Chervil has a more delicate taste than either our curly-leaved or flat-leaved Italian parsley, and chervil *(Anthriscus cerefolium)* is sometimes called French parsley. The feathery light green leaves resemble parsley, but the plant is smaller and never looks as robust.

Chervil seeds germinate and grow quickly, and the plant is very well-behaved in a pot or windowbox. It likes a rich, evenly moist potting soil, and while it needs plenty of light, will grow nicely without direct sun. Because chervil is a short-lived annual plant, keep the outer leaves pinched off for use while encouraging the new leaves unfolding in the center. When the indoor chervil plant turns yellow, its life is over and it is time to start more seed. I have had no luck coaxing an aged chervil plant along with fertilizer and good conversation. It is a plant with definite ideas about a proper life span.

Outdoor chervil is easy and rewarding to grow because it often reseeds itself. It is a cool weather herb, therefore, sow seed in a partially shaded spot with good drainage in late March (about the time early peas are planted). Then in late July plant a new crop of fall chervil. The autumn plants seem to have the best foliage, and they will provide fresh leaves even after a light frost.

Dried chervil is almost worthless! Use it fresh; however, it may be preserved by freezing it. Chop fresh leaves, pack in an ice cube tray, cover with water and freeze. Turn out frozen cubes to store in a plastic bag, thaw cubes as needed in a strainer and use the herb as fresh.

While fresh chervil is best known as a salad ingredient, it will turn a nondescript soup into something special. Stirred into butter, chervil is delicious as a spread or to use in broiling meat or fish. Add chopped chervil to an omelette. It can be substituted for parsley in almost any recipe. My mother-in-law steeps chervil in vermouth to pour over a roasting pork loin. The result is delectable!

Chervil has been grown in French and English herb gardens since it was first introduced by the Romans, but it is not so widely used in this country. Get to know chervil! It is said to make one youthful and to "comfort the cold stomach of the aged." Some European country people still nibble chervil to cure them of hiccups.

Keep a pot of the cheerful little plant growing in the kitchen during the winter and use it often. Be selective, though, as to whose plate gets the most chervil, because herbalist Gerard insisted that chervil "provoketh lust."

Allium schoenoprasum

Chives: Versatile & Rewarding

Everyone knows and uses chives! New herb gardeners are especially rewarded by the profusion of this hardy and versatile little herb.

As a member of the onion family, chives *(Allium schoenoprasum)* leaves are round and hollow. They look like miniature clumps of rushes. They can grow two feet tall, but are usually much smaller since the tops are continually cut and used.

Chives can be grown from seed, but it takes several seasons to get a sturdy clump. The best way to start chives is to find a friend with whom to share bulbs.

Chives are one of the best herbs for a winter window sill because they grow from a cluster of tiny white bulbs that do not mind living in a pot. Use good soil and feed them every few weeks with a weak natural fertilizer. Direct sun is best, but lots of light will do well for growing chives.

To complete their growing cycle, chives need a rest period. In February, put them outside to freeze for several weeks. Bring the pot back in, and new growth will sprout.

Plant the bulbs in your sunny garden next spring and divide the clumps in the fall.

Chopped chives make good garnishes for cream cheese mixtures, potatoes and eggs. They add a delicate onion flavor to soups, salads, and chopped meat dishes.

My children will spend a whole meal carefully discarding visible pieces of onion. But when I use chives, they get the mild onion flavor without seeing the source.

An interesting change of pace is to use chive butter for bread and vegetables.

Chive Butter

½ cup butter
1 tablespoon chopped chives
¼ tablespoon rosemary
1 tablespoon parsley
Cream the above mixture. Let the mixture mellow
for two or three hours before serving.

Chives are pretty enough to grow with your flowers. Round purple or pink clover-like blossoms appear in May and may continue all summer. For the ultimate in tender chives, keep the blossoms picked. However, I always enjoy leaving the flowers and my chives are fine.

Leaves can be harvested any time, and they freeze well. Snip the stalks into 1/4 inch lengths and freeze them in plastic sandwich bags. Although the flavor will be somewhat altered, chives can also be dried. Try drying the colorful chive blossoms as a winter feast for the eyes. Like all herbs, chives please more than one of our senses.

Chives have a lineage that is over 5000 years old. The modest little plant was pictured on Egyptian monuments. King Oberon's elfin troupe puffed on tiny pipes made of hollow chive leaves, and Roumanian gypsies used chives to tell fortunes.

Folk tradition advises us to eat leeks in winter, chives in May, and "all the year after, physicians may play."

*Coriandrum
umbelliferae*

One of the oldest herbs in use today is coriander *(Coriandrum umbelliferae)*. The lacy little plant must have loved the thin sandy soil of ancient Egypt where it grew wild. It was one of the spices found still recognizable in Egyptian tombs. The Romans later brought it to Europe where it came with them to England and then to America with English settlers.

The history of coriander is fascinating! Hippocrates used it as one of his mainstay medicinal herbs, and when it found its way to China, coriander was used in secret herbal mixtures to insure immortality. Biblical references to coriander seeds compare it to manna, the magical food God gave to the Israelites in the desert. (Exodus 16:31.)

Old herbals and literature mention coriander as an aphrodisiac, and it was once used by sorcerers, along with fennel, to conjure up the devil. I find this relationship with fennel interesting, because coriander will not grow any place near fennel in the garden.

The first year I grew coriander I kept smelling the most horrible stench as I weeded near the plants. I thought the cats had been in the herb garden again until I discovered the odor came from the coriander foliage itself. When I did a little research, I found I wasn't alone in my judgment. Ancient Pliny described coriander as that "very stinking herb," and the derivation of its name is the Greek word *koris,* which means "bug."

Not everyone shares this opinion of coriander's smell, though, because it is often used fresh in Spanish cooking where it is called "celantro." Many Indonesian dishes also contain dried coriander foliage, which seems to lose its strong scent when dried. In fact, the dried leaves smell a little like sage and lemon.

It is the large round seeds that are most flavorful and aromatic, however. They grow in umbel-heads like dill, and since they are so heavy, they must be picked as early as possible. Just as soon as the seeds turn a golden color they are ready. Once dried they last forever, and will still germinate in several years.

Crushed coriander seed is one of the ingredients in curry. Whole coriander seeds are often used in sausages and other chopped meat. Scandinavian bakers use coriander in cookies, gingerbread and pastries. Try adding a few coriander seeds to apple pie next time you make it. The flavor is very delicate and unusual.

Coriander is one of my favorite ingredients in potpourri. It adds spiciness without being as overpowering as cinnamon or cloves, and coriander retains its fragrance indefinitely.

If you want to grow coriander, plant the seeds in early spring in well-drained sunny soil. Be sure to plant the seeds where you want them to stay, because coriander will not transplant well. In June the lovely, faintly purple flowers appear, and the seeds should be ripe by August in our area. Leave a few to self-sow, and you will have a permanent coriander patch. Enjoy coriander's spicy fruit, respect its heritage, and don't blame its smell on the cats!

Foeniculum vulgare

Flattering Fennel

"Fennel is for flatterers," is the old English saying. The Italian phrase "Dare Finocchio" (to give fennel) actually means "to flatter." This symbolism was such common knowledge in Shakespeare's day in *Hamlet* that when Ophelia offered fennel to her brother, the audience immediately understood it was to warn him of flatterer's treachery.

Today fennel *(Foeniculum vulgare)* is known as that large garden herb which looks like celery and tastes like licorice. It is a biennial which can be grown as a perennial if the flower heads are kept pinched off each summer. In the Blue Ridge area it is best to dig up the long white tap roots in the fall. Be sure to leave three or four inches of stem attached. Store the roots in a cool humid cellar or outside in the cold frame. When spring comes, shorten the root a little and replant it in a warm sunny spot with excellent drainage. As an annual, fennel seeds should be planted in earliest spring. Fennel will not grow to its full size in one season when grown from seed, but this method is best in order to get feathery foliage or mature seeds for seasoning.

Florence fennel, called *finocchio* in Italy, is a second year plant with an enlarged pale base which is cooked like a vegetable. Tender leaves can be used to flavor fish, soups and salads. Seeds flavor breads, cakes, sauces, alcoholic drinks and are often chewed as breath fresheners. Harvest the seeds when they turn from green to yellow.

If you like licorice, try this recipe:

Sheila Howarth's Fennel Cookies

¾ cup butter
¾ cup sugar
1 egg yolk
2 cups flour
½ cup cornstarch
2 teaspoons fennel seed

Cream the butter and sugar. Beat in egg yolk. Sift the flour and cornstarch together. Then fold in the fennel seeds. Press the mixture into a 7 x 11 inch greased pan. Bake for half an hour (or until browned) at 350 degrees F. When cooled slightly, cut into strips. This makes about a dozen cookies.

Select a special place in the garden for fennel. It seems to have a harmful effect on bush beans, tomatoes, caraway and kohlrabi. Wormwood and coriander planted too closely to fennel will stunt its growth and prevent it from getting seed.

According to herbalist Culpepper, fennel ". . .expels wind, provokes urine and eases the pains of the stone." It was also traditionally used to "make people lean who are too fat," and those fasting on holy days would nibble fennel to curb their appetites. Nursing mothers drank barley water boiled with fennel seeds to increase the milk, and fennel was thought to improve failing eyesight. The dried foliage was sometimes used as a flea repellant.

In Greece fennel is a symbol of victory or success, and in northern Europe it was hung in homes to discourage evil. One early writer describes a festive hearth hung, "With aspen boughs and flowers and fennel gay."

Feverfew

Blooming in many country dooryards is the delicate daisy-like feverfew *(Chrysanthemum parthenium)*. Great-grandmother may have called it "bride's button" and carried it in her June wedding bouquet. It is one of the few herbs still loved and grown by almost every farm wife along the Blue Ridge, although she has long forgotten its original use.

In the past feverfew was grown close to the house to cleanse the air and ward off disease. When folks stopped keeping a little patch of herbs outside the door, feverfew made the jump to the Victorian flower garden, and it is still an old timey favorite in the perennial border.

Chrysanthemum
parthenium

Feverfew, sometimes also called featherfew, is a hardy perennial growing two or three feet. The leaves are light green, with a strong odor. In fact some botanists put it in the pyrethrum family *(Pyrethrum parthenium)* because of the sharp smell and burning sensation when tasted. The lovely flowers grow like clusters of small daisies which entirely cover the plant in June. If the plants are cut back when the bloom fades, they may bloom again in September.

Insects are never a problem on feverfew. To the contrary, it seems effective in discouraging insects from neighboring plants. Feverfew will grow in almost any soil with good drainage and at least a little sun. It is best to set out new plants or sow seed in early Spring. Then sit back and enjoy it, because feverfew is a hardy plant which requires no care. It will not spread to become a weedy pest.

Sometimes feverfew is confused with chamomile, but the yellow centers of feverfew blossoms are flat and the chamomile centers are conical. The sweet apple-like scent of chamomile could never be mistaken for the sharp scent of feverfew when the foliage of both is crushed.

Feverfew is a favorite in bouquets and cut flower arrangements because it does not readily wilt or drop its petals. In medieval monastary gardens feverfew was always grown in the "gardina sacristae" and used in the rites and decoration of the church as well as in making medicine.

Crushed feverfew leaves are still used to relieve the sting of insect bites, and a wash of leaves is said to ward off insects when rubbed on the skin.

In Finland feverfew was once given as a tonic for consumption, and the herbalist Parkinson claimed it provided relief for opium addicts suffering from an overdose. One of feverfew's folk names of "Maydes Weed" refers to its traditional use as a "general strengthener of the womb," according to the herbalist Culpeper. Its most common name of feverfew comes from the virtue of driving off fever. Herbalist Gerard in 1633 wrote that when bound to one's wrists, it would protect against the ague. He also advised wine steeped with feverfew and applied to the head would purge a siege of melancholy.

No wonder our forebearers felt secure with a clump of feverfew outside the door. Grow some for its homey beauty and distinguished heritage. It may even draw the fairies to dance in your garden, because according to English writer Nora Hopper, it is a favorite of the wee folk who dance

"So light and true, that they shake no dew,
From featherfew . . . . ."

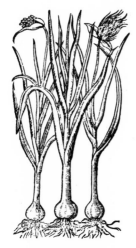

Allium liliaceae

Good Garlic Wards Away Evil Spirits

Early autumn seems to be the best time to plant garlic *(Allium liliaceae).* Take a plump firm garlic bulb and divide it into separate cloves. Plant them two inches deep, five inches apart, in single or double rows—in the vegetable garden, please! Garlic, with its infinite variety of uses, is just too coarse and rank for the noble herb garden. Its plain straggly top will detract from the beauty of your herbs, and its strong smell will overpower the delicate herbal scents. Harvest the bulbs of garlic in early October when the tops die down. Garlic needs a long, warm growing season, so autumn-planted bulbs do better. Store garlic for the winter in an open mesh bag in a cool dry spot.

There is a legend that when Satan stepped out of the Garden of Eden after the fall of man, garlic sprang up from the spot where he placed his left foot and onion from the spot where he placed his right foot. Garlic has appeared in literature and folk legend from ancient Egypt to the present day. Homer credits garlic with saving Ulysses from being turned into a pig by Circe; and it is still a Mediterranean folk symbol as protection against evil. My husband's Roman ancestors would be pleased to see the handsome string of braided garlic hanging in our kitchen to keep away dark spirits and to add flavor and health to our meals.

Garlic is such a common seasoning that its uses are almost unlimited. If you are a novice in using garlic, remember to go slowly at first. Try rubbing the salad bowl with a sliced clove of garlic, adding a little finely chopped garlic to the soup pot or inserting a few peeled garlic cloves into meat for roasting. Grow your own and use the chopped green tops in salad. As your taste for garlic increases, become more bold.

What about garlic breath? Try chewing on fresh parsley or drinking milk after a garlic rich meal. Better yet, make sure everyone in the household eats garlic too.

It is the potent smell of garlic that makes it so valuable in herbal remedies. The essential oil contains allicin, and there is a great deal of current research which indicates garlic may indeed be an effective antiseptic and valuable in lowering blood pressure.

Garlic is also useful to organic gardeners as either a companion plant to insect-prone vegetables or as the major ingredient in a homemade insect spray. I discourage aphids with a spray made of a quart of water, three garlic cloves and a tablespoon of hot red pepper all whirred up together in a blender. Strain the mixture, put it in an old Windex bottle and attack the invaders. Bugs do not like the smell either.

Enjoy your garlic, but follow Shakespeare's advice and do not use it when you want to make a good impression. "And, most dear actors, eat no onions nor garlic, for we are to utter sweet breath."

Scented Geraniums

As Victorian as gingerbread porches, scented geraniums are a nostalgic piece of living Americana. In 1880 the most remote farm house probably had several varieties crowded on the window sill. Even today a cold, sunny window requires a pot or two of the beautiful aromatic plants.

A member of the same pelargonium family as the showy red geraniums, scented geraniums produce not only tiny modest flowers but a whole range of wonderful scents. One crushed leaf will sweeten an entire room.

Scented geraniums have a favored sunny spot in my garden and are a key ingredient in my potpourri. Before frost, I take cuttings for house plants or sometimes dig up the whole plant to bring inside.

A little lemon-scented "Prince Rupert" variety grows by my kitchen sink, and each evening the warm steam from washing dishes releases the spicy citrus fragrance.

Seventeenth century sailors first brought home scented geraniums as souvenirs from the South African Cape. By 1870 there were over 150 varieties listed in American seed catalogs.

There is as much variety in leaf shape and texture as in scents. Leaves can be shaped like oak leaves, pheasants' feet, curly ruffles, grape leaves or umbrellas. Some are velvety, some sticky or even prickly to touch.

Just a few of the scents are rose *(P. graveolens)*, nutmeg *(P. fragrans)*, lemon *(P. crispum)*, lime *(P. nevosum)* and mint *(P. quercifolium)*. Many have delicious combination scents like lemon-rose.

Our great-grandmothers soaked leaves in alcohol or vinegar to make sweet water for bathing an aching head. Loosening corset laces may have worked better for them, and gulping Excedrin may relieve our headaches, but bathing one's brow in sweet water always sounds so much more fun.

If you are not prone to swooning, there are other wonderful uses for scented geraniums. Place a leaf in the bottom of your apple jelly. Dry leaves for sachets, potpourri or tea.

Spread a layer of rose geranium leaves on the bottom of your greased and floured cake pan before pouring in a plain white or yellow cake batter. The delicate flavor spreads throughout the cake while it bakes. Do not forget to discard the leaves when you remove the cake from its pan. Pick fresh leaves for a garnish.

Scented geraniums grow well under the same conditions as your regular zonal geraniums. Plenty of sunshine and not too much water are the main factors. I have never had insect pests on my scented geraniums—so that is another one of their merits.

Outside, they will grow to the size of a shrub in one season, and in a pot, as large as you permit. Put a large tub of scented geraniums in a spot where you will brush against it often to release the scent.

Share slips with your neighbors, and make it a tradition to give visiting children a spicy fresh-smelling leaf with which to play. They will be fascinated by its odor, texture and shape.

Hen and Chicks

Sempervivum tectorum

Almost every country family has an old tub of hen-and-chicks growing near the back door. It is that succulent little sedum plant with thick fleshy rosettes which quickly spread by producing miniatures all around. But did you know that hen-and-chicks *(Sempervivum tectorum)* has a long and distinguished history?

The ancient civilization of Crete records the first use of hen-and-chicks. The fascinating names people have given the little plant show how widely it was valued. In England and America alone it is variously called old man-and-woman, house leeks, stonecrop, wall-pepper, Jupiter's beard, and sengreene.

Folk remedies for burns, sore eyes and slow-healing skin blemishes often include houseleeks. The leaves are fat and filled with a soothing juice very much like the well-known exotic Aloe vera. Herbalist Gerard confirms that physicians in the 16th century were prescribing houseleeks for "creeping ulcers, rheumatike," and mixed with barley meal applied to "take away the paine of goute."

Because houseleeks seem to thrive by growing on top of things like   stone walls and roof tops, it was thought to protect houses from lightning. A charm for fishermen, found in an old book by Albert Magnus, includes houseleeks. According to "Le petit Albert, " if you put nettles, clover, houseleek juice, corn water, thyme and marjoram into a fish net, the net will immediately fill with fish.

With such outstanding virtues, why not find a place in the herb garden for houseleeks? The sedum family will grow in spots for which you have given up hope. They require good drainage, sun and little else. They will thrive on poor soil and almost no water - usually spreading quickly. In addition to the common hen-and-chicks variety, there is a cooly one called *Sempervivum arachnoideum.* It produces a cob-webbed effect and has dense clusters of red flowers. There are creeping sedums, called prickmadams in the old days, which will cascade over stone walls or grow between paving stones.

Houseleeks will stay green almost all winter in the Blue Ridge area, and the blossoms are always interesting. *Sempervivum spathulifolium* makes a nice ground cover with yellow flowers. *Sempervivum spectabile* "meteor" has showy red flowers. Gerard said they always bloom "after the Summer Solstice," and he is still right.

Our grandmothers forgot some of the reasons for loving these homey little plants, but they still grew them. Carry on the tradition and use the soothing leaves for simple remedies. Remember, also, the houseleek's heritage as its beauty is enjoyed.

Marrubium vulgare

Hardy, Historical Horehound

One herb that will remain green under the snow is horehound *(Marrubium vulgare).* Small tufts of wrinkled leaves will sprout at the base of old dry stalks from last summer. One sturdy plant usually provides enough foliage to brew up a pleasant tasting cough syrup or horehound drops for a small family.

Horehound has been used as a medicine since the days of ancient Egypt when it wa⁵ called the seed of

94

Horus. In addition of its traditional use of soothing a cough, it has been used as an antidote for plant poisons and as a folk remedy for the bite of a mad dog. All of the old herbalists praised its vitures highly.

Gerard tells us that horehound grew wild in the rough and barren places of Europe at the time it was being introduced to England. He wrote, "My kinde friend Mr. Buckner, an Apothecary of London the last year beeing 1632, found the plant gorwing wilde in Oxfordshire in the field joining to Witney Park a mile from the Towne." I wonder if it still grows there?

Horehound was one of the five plants stated by the Mishna to be bitter herbs, which the Jews were ordered to take for the Feast of Passover. In fact, the botanical name *Marrubium* is supposed to come from the Hebrew word Marrob, a bitter juice.

Horehound likes a sunny spot and will thrive in poor shallow soil as long as it is well-drained. Fertilizer and mulch are wasted on horehound, and its characteristic musky aroma is even stronger when the plant is neglected. The best way to start horehound is to sow seeds indoors in early spring or to purchase a plant from a nursery. Cuttings can be taken in the spring to propagate horehound. Self-sown seedlings are not uncommon, although if the leaves are harvested regularly, the plant should not bloom. It is a perennial which winters over well here in the Blue Ridge, but in areas with harsher winters, like New England, horehound must be treated as an annual.

Horehound is a pretty little plant to grow in a place that is usually scraggly or bare. It also makes an interesting potted plant for a winter windowsill or greenhouse.

It is fun brewing up your own cough mixtures, and it is probably as effective as any non-prescription cough syrup.

Old-fashioned Horehound Drops

Combine the horehound tea with two cups of sugar a pinch of cream of tartar. Cook the mixture over low heat until a drop will become hard in a glass of cold water. Pour the mixture in a buttered shallow plate and score into little squares when half-hardened. When completely cooled, break into pieces and store in a cool, dry place.

Hyssop: The Plant of Fresh Starts

Hyssopus officionalis

In my Harpers Ferry herb garden, hyssop *(Hyssopus officionalis)* is a 24-inch evergreen shrub with a haze of purple-blue flowers all summer until frost. During the winter the compact shape gives form to the garden and the tiny dark green leaves add color.

When spring cleaning is finished, bring a bowl of fresh hyssop inside the house. It is the traditional biblical plant of cleansing and purification. Include a sprig of hyssop in a bouquet for new parents, newlyweds or anyone beginning a new venture. Hyssop is the plant of fresh starts! In one of the Psalms, David says "purge me with hyssop and I shall be clean."

The whole plant exudes a pleasant odor like that of rosemary or savory, but with a hint of camphor. During the Middle Ages, it was commonly used like parsley in cooking. Hyssop was chopped or sprinkled on roasting meat or added to soups and stews. The flavor is not very popular today, except in the Midi area of France where it is still used in farm kitchens. It is quite tart with a definite bite to it, but the colorful mild tasting flowers decorate a salad and the virtues of hyssop are constant.

Today hyssop tea (with lemon and honey) is a good cough remedy. The herbalist Parkinson loved it. He called the homely herb "more easy for the parson's purse and more familiar for all men's bodies." Hyssop water (cold tea) is said to be good for one's complexion when used externally. It is also one of the oldest home remedies for a black eye when used as a leaf compress. Pour a quart of boiling water over a half cup of crushed leaves and allow it to steep for five or six minutes to make hyssop tea. Use twice as many leaves to brew a skin lotion.

Bees and butterflies are attracted to hyssop flowers, but hyssop never seems troubled by insects or plant diseases. In fact, old gardening books often recommended planting hyssop near grapes for healthier vines. Modern companion-planting gardeners use hyssop to lure the cabbage butterfly from the cabbages.

A low hyssop hedge is spectacular; and hyssop is the perfect plant for a knot garden. The best way to start hyssop is to purchase a small plant in early spring. Seeds can be started indoors and then set out in April, but seedlings must be coddled the first season - no weeds and lots of mulch. After the plant is established, it can be increased by stem cuttings in June or July. Hyssop needs a well-drained soil, prefers full sun and like most herbs, thrives in a slightly alkaline soil. My hyssop grows happily, however, in partial shade near a row of lavender.

Lady's Mantle—An April Star

Alchemilla vulgaris

By summer my little cluster of Lady's Mantle *(Alchemilla vulgaris)* is almost hidden by the showier herbs around it, but in early April, Lady's Mantle is the star. As soon as the winter mulch is cleared away, bright green leaves unfold in tiny pleats. Herbalist Gerard described the unusual leaves of Lady's Mantle as "round with five or six corners finely indented about the edges, which before they be opened are plaited and folded together" not unlike the bodice of a lady's gown.

It is one of the herbs which our forebears thought lovely enough to dedicate to the Virgin Mary. Before the Middle Ages, and even today in some parts of France, it is called *Pied de Lyon* or Lion's Paw.

The exquisite leaves grow almost flat on the ground and in the early morning one drop of dew collects in the center of each leaf. Dawn was the hour when dew was thought to have magical powers, and there surely must still be magic in those droplets of liquid silver. Folk tradition says if a girlchild's face is washed with this dew of Lady's Mantle, she will grow into a beautiful lady.

The flowers of Lady's Mantle are delicate and yellow growing on upright stems. They look almost like baby's breath and dry just as well for winter bouquets or wreaths. When a whole bed of Lady's Mantle is blooming, it looks like a sunny yellow mist.

The little plant will tolerate either sun or partial shade. It does like good drainage, sweet soil and room to spread out. It is an excellent plant for a rock garden or even a ground cover on banks or slopes. Gerard was very specific in describing where Lady's Mantle grew in 1633. I wonder if it still can be found growing "upon the banke of a mote that incloseth house in Bushey called Bourn Hall, fourteen miles from London in the high way to Watford?"

In old herb gardens Lady's Mantle was often grown right in among the creeping thymes. There is a smaller Lady's Mantle with silver leaves called *Alchemilla alpina* which you may enjoy growing for a color variation. Both varieties reproduce by sending out runners like strawberry plants. Although Lady's Mantle does bloom and set seed, I have never seen seedlings come up.

Although Lady's Mantle was once a valued medicinal herb, it is almost never used any longer in our country or England. In Switzerland, though, the dried leaves are still brewed into a tea for many minor discomforts. Its properties are said to be very much like chamomile, and the taste is very mild.

Lavandula

Lavender

Who can hear the word lavender without thinking of soft mauve color and delicate scents? Lavender *(Lavandula)* has been part of our heritage since it was first brought to England by the Romans who enjoyed its clean scent in washing water, soap and perfume. The little herb found a pleasant home in the mild English climate, and then came to this country with the first settlers. According to an English garden book by Leonard Meager, seventeenth century colonist John Winthrop directed the planting of his gardens; Winthrop listed lavender as an herb one must grow and cut often.

Today lavender is responsible for one of the largest herbal industries in the world. Hundreds of acres of lavender are grown in France and England. The spikes of lavender flowers (often called Spike in old herbals) are harvested and dried just as the buds open. They give off a wonderful refreshing aroma for years; therefore, they have become an important ingredient of potpourri, perfumes, sweet bags or soaps.

Lavender grows well if it is given a sunny location with protection from the wind. My healthiest lavender grows on the south side of the house tucked into the base of an old limestone foundation. The plant thrives in rather poor soil if there is a neutral to alkaline pH level. Never mulch lavender. An elderly Harpers Ferry lady once warned me to keep the ground bare under lavender, so it won't "choke." The plant likes a warm dry soil.

It is almost impossible to grow lavender from seed. The tiny black seeds take months to germinate and then grow slowly and are so vulnerable for the first year that they almost never thrive outdoors. Start with a three or four inch lavender plant. A cutting taken in July will be ready for a permanent spot by autumn. Stem cuttings will root best if taken in midsummer, placed in damp sand and kept in a light, but shady place for a few weeks.

Keep the bloom cut in order to have several flowerings a season. The leaves are also aromatic and often harvested for potpourri or for making lavender oil.

There are several varieties of lavender. *Lavandula vera* is one of the tallest (two or three feet) and the most aromatic. It is the traditional English lavender and grows well in my area. *Lavandula spica* produces a greater volume of flowers, but is less aromatic. *Lavandula stoechas* smells more like rosemary and is less winter-hardy. The Munstead variety is a low growing plant and is good for a flower border.

Traditionally, lavender has been used to create sweet scents in our surroundings. Remember grandmother's lavender-scented sheets? Lavender's medicinal use was to cure diseases of head and "comfort the braine very well." Herbalist Turner suggested stitching it up in caps to be worn on the head. Shakespeare uses the term "hat lavender" in several of his plays.

Use your imagination with lavender, but grow and enjoy it. Although I have never tried it, Queen Elizabeth I was said to love lavender conserve. I have discovered, however, that a few lavender buds slipped into the pot when brewing either china or herb tea will make a ho-hum tea magnificent!

Lemon Verbena

Lemon verbena *(Lippia citriodora)* needs to come indoors before frost. It is a very sensitive herb, and even the cool evenings before a frost may damage it.

Despite its prima donna termperament, it remains one of my favorites. The long, slender leaves are full of the clean scent and taste of fresh lemon, and the essence of the dried leaves last almost forever.

Lemon verbena is a native American aristocrat of herbs that was carried to Europe and North America by Spanish conquistadores. According to legend, only the ruling families of Mexico and Guatemala were permitted to grow and use lemon verbena before the Spanish arrived. Today the elegant plant thrives throughout Central and South America - often growing as tall as an apple tree. Because lemon verbena's European heritage is so short compared to that of most herbs, its uses in the kitchen and on the apothecary shelf are not as well known.

The leaves are best dried individually in order not to lose or crush a single one. They will curl almost completely and dry in a day or two.

Lemon verbena tea is delicious even to those who are not fond of herb teas. Use a teaspoon of crushed leaves for each cup of tea. Steep it ten minutes in the pot. It is said to help settle a disturbed stomach.

My potpourri is never complete without lemon verbena, and the leaves alone are nice for a sachet. Men seem to enjoy the scent because it is neither floral nor sweet. Combine dried lemon verbena leaves, lemon balm leaves and orris root for a citrus potpourri. Some dried marigolds or calendula blossoms will add yellow color.

Lemon verbena is deciduous and will naturally lose its leaves in the fall - even though it is in the house and given lots of loving attention. The first year I grew it I was so disappointed to see the leaves fall; however, I watered the stick hopefully and in early winter new leaves appeared. During cold weather, it is a good idea to take the potted lemon verbena in the warm shower with you once a week to keep spider mites from invading it. A heavenly scent will be an added shower pleasure.

In warm, sunny weather lemon verbena will flourish outside. Mine usually grows three or four feet tall and just as wide. It rarely blooms in the Blue Ridge and **never sets** seed. Cuttings taken in April or May sometimes root, but patience is the watchword.

The haughty lady, Herba Luisa, as lemon verbena is called in South America, gives a scent unparalleled in the plant world, so she is worth a little pampering.

Lovage Flourishes

Levisticum officinale

There is a five foot explosion of green in the herb garden! It is lovage *(Levisticum officinale),* a vigorous lush plant with leaves and stems which taste very much like celery.

One plant is more than enough for a family since it often grows as tall as a basketball player and seems to thrive on cutting. Fresh leaves minced in potato salad or a tossed salad are wonderful. The flavor is a little more peppery than celery and is even better in soups or stews. Sometimes the stems are blanched and eaten as a vegetable dish. In England the seeds are often used in candies, cordials and even in some tobacco blends.

Lovage is a native of the Balkan countries and the Mediterranean shores. It now grows wild on the seashore in Scotland and Northumberland where it was first brought by the Romans. American colonists brought it over early, and it was a favorite in 18th century herb gardens.

Seventeenth century herbalist Gerard says "The roots . . . cleareth the sight and putteth it away all spots, freckles and redness of the face." American folk tradition calls on lovage as a soothing gargle for sore throats.

Lovage is a hardy perennial lasting twenty years or more. It is also very easy to grow. Sow seeds directly in the ground in late summer, and they will be hearty little plants by next spring. Almost any spot would be acceptable for lovage, but because it is so tall, a corner is usually best. Sometimes lovage makes a good focal point in the center of an herb garden, however. The only place lovage will not thrive is a very hot and dry spot. It prefers fertile soil and a little shade, but it tolerates less than perfect conditions very nicely. Although the plant is large, it is tidy and never spreads out like mint to become pesty.

Lovage dries well and can be cut back two or three inches from the ground in early fall without hurting the plant at all. Since the stems are so fleshy, remove the leaves and spread them out in an arid, dark place to dry. Then store them in tightly capped jars. Lovage is an excellent ingredient for seasoning soups and stews.

Dried Herb Mixture for Seasoning Winter Soups and Stews

Dried herbs used for seasoning winter soups and stews include lovage, parsley, thyme, calendula blossoms, and a pinch of dill and rosemary.

Grow this exuberant herb for its beauty, flavor, and healthfulness. The next time you meet your lover, wear lovage around your neck - it is said to inspire everlasting devotion.

Melissa officinalis

Melissa the Consoling

The wonderful scent of lemon balm *(Melissa officinalis)* makes it one of the most loved and useful summer herbs. The fresh leaves are good for punch, fruit desserts and as garnish or seasoning for seafood. Hanging bunches of lemon balm in a room will fill it with cool lemony scents. Sometimes lemon balm is rubbed on fine furniture to polish and scent the wood. The oils are distilled for perfume and dried leaves are a main ingredient in many potpourris.

Lemon balm is a native of the mountainous section of southern Europe but the hardy perennial will grow well in the Blue Ridge as well. In fact it will spread profusely, but because it is so useful, one rarely can have too much lemon balm. The bright green leaves are oval, toothed and slightly hairy. Outside it will grow to a lush round bush three feet tall and wide; and inside it will grow to almost a foot. The flowers are small and white, but if they are picked often, lemon balm will not bloom at all.

Balm, as it was traditionally called, will grow in almost any soil, but will thrive in a well-drained spot with partial shade. Seeds can be sown directly in the soil in early spring or started in peat pots at any time for houseplants. Do not lose patience, because germination often takes several weeks. Once the lemon balm is established, root divisions or stem cuttings are the easiest way to propagate.

Melissa, the Linnean name of lemon balm, means "bee" in Greek. When in bloom, it is one of the favorite plants of bees; old-time beekeepers would often rub the inside of bee-skeps with lemon balm to attract new swarms.

Cows are also supposed to love lemon balm; and if it is planted in pastures, it is said to increase milk yields.

Lemon balm is a consoling herb. The virtue of the plant to bloom and thrive even after severe shocks was thought to impart those qualities to people. There was once a "restorative cordial" called Carmelite water which was made primarily of lemon balm and angelica.

Although lemon balm is best used when fresh, it can easily be dried. Pick bushy stems just before they flower and hang in loose bunches in a dry shade place for a few days. Attics or clean dry sheds are perfect places to dry herbs. If the weather is damp and the balm does not dry within a few days, strip the leaves off the stems and spread them thinly on a cookie sheet in the oven with the lowest setting. Unless balm leaves dry quickly, they will turn black and lose much of their scent and flavor. Store in a tightly closed container in a cool, dry and dark spot.

Why not spread balm butter on broiled meat for a slightly different flavor?

Balm Butter

Combine four tablespoons butter with freshly ground pepper with two tablespoons chopped lemon balm leaves.

Lemon balm is traditional with mint for cooling the summer heat by making refreshing drinks, decorating the house or wearing fresh sprigs. Use it freely!

Fine Green Mint

Mint

"Mints spread like weeds, and we never use them anyway." Have you ever muttered those words as you pulled long mint runners out of the flower bed?

It is true mints have no respect for the territorial rights of other plants, but once you start using them in a hundred different ways, you may find mints will not grow fast enough.

From earliest times people noticed mints sweetened the air and cleared the senses. They were strewn among the foul smelling rushes laid on medieval castle and cottage floors. Mint was thrown in the paths of victorious warriors.

From India comes the old custom of hanging bunches of mint by doors and open windows to make breezes smell fresher.

Concoct your own tooth powder or mouthwash with mint. Combine baking soda with dried powdered mint leaves to clean your teeth, and steep fresh mint leaves in sherry for a superb-tasting mouthwash.

Most general cookbooks will have plenty of traditional recipes for using mint with lamb or new peas. Throw a few mint leaves in the pot with carrots or new potatoes next time you serve them. Try adding a tablespoon of dried mint and parsley to your meatballs or meatloaf for a mideastern flavor.

Slip a mint leaf in your apple jelly. Steep mint leaves in vinegar. Add a pinch of mint to any cool summer drink or enjoy it solo, brewed as a tea. Orange mint is my favorite in the teapot.

One of my three favorites is spearmint, "Mentha spicata." It is the largest and most common mint. If you are not sure which variety is in your garden, it is probably spearmint or a near relative. The leaves are dark green, finely serrated and almost shiny.

Orange mint, "Mentha citrata," has round, smooth edges leaves and a distinctive rich citrus aroma. As tea or in a potpourri, it is wonderful. Dry some for a jar on your desk because it is said sniffing mint will increase one's brainpower.

Applemint, "Mentha rotundifolia," has smaller light green fuzzy leaves and an apple smell. It needs a protected corner of the garden to winter over, but the extra effort is worth it.

In mythology, Mintha, mint's namesake, was a beautiful nymph who loved Pluto, god of the underworld. In a jealous rage, Persephone changed her into the small mint plant. Since then mints have lived in the shady places of the dark world of Pluto.

That may be why mints will thrive in rich, humus soil with shady dampness. They will, however, survive almost any place.

If spreading mints upset your sense of garden orderliness, encircle their roots with metal strips at least twelve inches deep or give them an out-of-the-way place all to themselves.

I just thin out my mint patch two or three times a season, and it has never been a problem. In fact, I never seem to have enough mint.

Cherish your mints, value their long rich heritage and echo the old London street cry, "Come see my mint, my fine green mint."

Origanum vulgare

Oregano - an Herbal Mountain Joy

"Joy of the mountains" is the Greek name for oregano *(Origanum vulgare)*. The sweet spicy herb could just as easily claim the title "joy of the kitchen." Spaghetti sauce or Mexican food just cannot be made without oregano. It is a zesty herb for hearty winter dishes.

Between the parsley and garlic powder in most American kitchens will be found an old jar of dried up oregano. It is hard to recognize as the luxuriant rosy-blooming plant which

105

spills over the walk in my herb garden.

Grow and become familiar with oregano. Closely related to sweet or knotted marjoram *(Origanum majorana)*, it is a small-leaved low growing perennial herb. Herbalists always seem to be arguing over whether *true oregano* has white, lavender or pink flowers. I have had seed from the same plant produce progeny with all three flowers. However, the most important family virtue, a pungent taste, is common to them all.

Full sun, dry, slightly alkaline soil and good drainage will make an oregano plant happy. Seeds germinate well outside in warm soil, and root cuttings from established plants usually do well. For a bushy, compact plant, keep the new growth pinched back after June. In the Blue Ridge area, though, I have found oregano will spread into a lovely cascade and bloom all season if left unpinched. For harvesting, I cut an entire stem - instead of only the tips of several.

Oregano dries quickly and keeps its flavor well. It is one of the few herbs which can be dried in the sun. The concentration of oils is probably greater than that of any other herb. Home grown and carefully stored oregano is spicier and hotter than the commercial herb. It is well worth the effort!

What effort? Such a pretty little plant should be grown regardless of the kitchen. On hot, sunny days, the cut blossoms give a delicate beauty and scent indoors. Oregano flowers dry to a sturdy red-brown color and are perfect for herb wreaths or dried arrangements in the fall.

Oregano has an ancient medicinal heritage - used both internally and externally. With a hotness akin to chili powder, however, I cannot imagine drinking oregano tea. One herbalist, however, wrote that it can be made into a drink "which is extremely grateful." Most old home remedies recommend oregano externally as a linament or for a toothache poultice.

Traditionally, it was a strewing herb to keep dank castle or cottage floors sweet-smelling. Seventeenth century herbalist John Parkinson wrote Origanum was ". . .put in nosegays and in the window of houses, as also in sweete pouders, sweete bags and sweete washing waters . . .Our daintiest women doe put it to still among their sweet herbes."

While eating a spicy pizza, take note of the little herb. Oregano is a symbol of honor in many countries, and it has been highly prized for longer than mankind remembers.

Cold-Defying Parsley

Parsley

From my second story window the winter herb garden looks like a geometric rug of rich browns, beige and mahogany. Only a spot of electric green jars my eye: cold-defying parsley. It is still fresh and abundant.

There is no need to nurse along a winter potted parsley plant when outside under the snow, parsley will almost always give up a handful of green leaves.

Everyone recognizes parsley, but its versatility and effectiveness are often overlooked. Always eat the sprig of parsley garnishing your plate. It has more Vitamin C than an orange and is rich in calcium and vitamin A.

Parsley has been used and cultivated so long that its origins have been forgotten. The ancient Greeks believed Hercules was partial to parsley and used it for athletic victory garlands.

Almost every culture has superstitions connected with parsley. In some parts of England it is thought planting parsley brings bad luck. My theory is that folk legends abound because the seed takes unusually long to germinate. It is said the tiny seeds have to travel to the Devil and back nine times before they sprout. My Appalachian grandmother insisted upon planting parsley on Good Friday.

Another adage warns never to transplant parsley or bad luck will be the result. Actually, parsley has a very long tap root and just does not transplant well.

Parsley was often planted on graves. Hence the saying "in great need of parsley" actually meant "at death's door." In Greece where parsley and rue often border the garden the saying "Oh, we are only at parsley and rue," means a proposed undertaking has not yet been started.

Parsley is a biennial which grows easily and provides an abundance of green leaves. Use them fresh in all salads, with almost any mixture of herbs. Fresh leaves also make a fine-tasting, healthy diuretic tea. According to the old herbalists, parsley would cure almost any ailment and even prevent baldness - if the powdered seed were sifted on one's head occasionally.

Chewing fresh parsley will make a sweet breath even for a confirmed garlic eater.

Parsley Sauce

1½ cups dry white wine
4 tablespoons chopped fresh parsley
¾ cup chicken broth

Combine the above ingredients in a saucepan and simmer for 15 minutes. Serve over new potatoes or carrots.

Humus and moist soil is best for growing parsley. Seeds sown early and shallow in full sun do best. Since the seedlings take a while to get sturdy, it is important to keep the weeds down at first. Although parsley will live for two years, in the second year it is more interested in setting seed than producing foliage. Plant seeds each spring for a few seasons and soon the parsley row will reseed annually.

The prettiest parsley is the curly-leaved *Petroselinum crispum*, but I prefer the more flavorful flat leaved or Italian parsley, *Petroselinum crispum latifolium.*

Both kinds store well if the leaves are dried quickly and stored in a dark place to retain the bright green color. The best way to dry parsley is to spread the leaves thinly on a cookie sheet in a warm oven until they are crisp.

This beautiful herb still brings the pleasure it did in 1440 when "Perselye" deserved a whole chapter in Mayster Ion Gardener's book. Even then ". . .being green it serveth to lay upon sundry meates."

Pot Marigolds

Calendula officinalis

Old fashioned pot marigolds open golden orange blossoms to the sun each morning and close them with the sunset. They are calendulas *(Calendula officinalis)*, and not to be confused with the African or French marigolds commonly used today to brighten up the flower bed or discourage bugs from the vegetable garden.

Pot marigolds are hardy annuals whose cheerful flowers will continue until the thermometer drops below 25° degrees F. In Europe they often bloom in each month of the year. Hence, their generic Latin name calendula for *"Calends,"* first day of each month.

The history of this showy herb is filled with symbolism and poetry. The ancients observed its sensitivity to the sun and the way it followed the path of the sun each day, much like its larger cousin the sunflower. Allusions are made to it in the literature of ancient Egypt, Greece and Rome. In Europe medieval ladies wore posies of marigolds to symbolize happiness and it was often used in heraldry. Charles I dejectedly wrote "The marigold observes the sun, More than my subjects me have done." Shakespeare uses marigolds as a favorite metaphor.

The common name of marigold comes from a time in medieval Europe when it was common to dedicate beautiful things to the Virgin, and the calendula bloomed on every festival in her honor in England.

The healing properties of marigolds were common knowledge to our ancestors, and the old herbalists describe its effectiveness in relieving fever, sore eyes, skin irritations and "trembling of the harte." It is the flower petals which are gathered for both medicinal and culinary use. One legend tells us the person gathering calendula petals must be free of deadly sin and must say three Pater Nosters and Aves. After gathering the petals that person will be able to recognize a thief. In more modern times, calendula petals have been used as a soothing tea and made into ointment for dressing small wounds. During the Civil War and World War I, calendula petals were used to control bleeding.

In the kitchen calendula has many more pleasant uses. Fresh petals are delicious in a salad and give beautiful color to a bowl of greens. I dry the petals and store them to use in winter soups and stews. They give a rich golden color and add a pleasant flavor. In fact, calendula was often used as a substitute for the expensive saffron.

Calendulas are the brightest herbs in the garden. Flowers are often four inches across with petals like the rays of the sun (a member of the *Compositae* family) and in every color from pale sunrise yellow to the vivid orange of sunset. Plant the seeds outside in a sunny spot after the last frost of spring. They will begin to bloom in June and continue well into December if you pick flowers regularly. Burpee Seed Co. has developed a shorter compact calendula with large abundant flowers which does well in small gardens.

To dry, simply pull off the petals, lay them on paper in a dark dry spot, and then store in a tight container when they are crisp.

Enjoy the noble marigolds, and give them an open corner of the garden where they can worship the sun in their time-honored way. Remember John Keats' beautiful ode to them in "I Stood Tiptoe Upon a Little Hill" (1817).

> "Open fresh your round of
>   starry folds,
> Ye ardent marigolds!
> Dry up the moisture from your
>   gold lids,

Rosmarinus officinalis

Rosemary for Remembrance

The Christmas herb is rosemary. With a heritage of more legend, ritual and poetry than any other herb, rosemary *(Rosmarinus officinalis)* was cherished even before the first Christmas. This most aristocratic of herbs goes hand-in-hand with our most festive holiday.

The traditional Christmas boar's head was always brought "crested with bays and rosemary." Because rosemary is evergreen, it was used to deck the halls. But in northern Europe and England only a few sprigs could be spared to tuck in with the abundant holly and pine.

Rosemary is a native of sunny Mediterranean shores, and the stunted northern transplants had to be brought inside or protected during cold winters. It was brought to England by the Romans, to northern Europe by Charles the Great, and Captain John Mason brought it to Virginia in the 17th century.

On Sicily and the southern coast of France and Italy, rosemary grows eight feet tall. In Greece it grows wild. We know it as a small gray shrub, and it will thrive only when we try to recreate its native growing conditions. *Rosmarinus,* its Latin name, means "dew of the sea."

Grow rosemary in a pot outside in summer and bring it in before frost. Water it sparingly and give it a well drained soil like the Mediterranean's arid shore. Never let rosemary dry out completely, however. It is unforgiving! It will drop every leaf and die.

Give rosemary lots of sun and keep the top well misted to resemble gentle shoreline fogs and you will be rewarded with lovely blue flowers.

Rosemary can be grown from seed, but it takes several years to reach a few inches. The best way to start a new plant is from a cutting taken in mid-summer.

Rosemary is for remembrance. Sprigs are often exchanged as symbolic tokens, and brides carry rosemary in their bouquets. Small rosemary trees are often decorated for Christmas. Rosemary twigs are tied to cradles to insure sweet dreams for little children, and balding grandfathers drink rosemary tea to encourage good memory and a full shock of hair.

We are most familiar with rosemary in the kitchen. I always use it chopped and sprinkled over roast beef or pork, and it is the traditional herb for lambs. To me rosemary's flavor is like a combination of nutmeg, pine, and ginger.

Rosemary Baked Potatoes

Make rosemary baked potatoes by slicing a potato lengthways in half and rubbing the cut surface with chopped rosemary. Place face down on a greased baking sheet and bake for 45 minutes at 400° F.

Try substituting rosemary for sage in the Christmas turkey stuffing!

Rue – The Herb of Grace

Rue is a delicate-looking little plant that belies its powerful history. For the first time, I am growing rue *(Rue graveolens)* on my window sill, and beginning to know it well as a winterbound companion.

Rue is growing inside this year because it brought me a new friend. One day last summer a frantic woman called looking for fresh rue to feed her son's prize caterpillar. It seemed this finicky insect ate only rue, and her plant was completely defoliated. Someone had told her of my herb garden. I had an old half-forgotton rue plant someplace, so I told her to come on over. In ten minutes, she was here, and we were crawling through weeds to strip rue leaves for the greedy little worm. My rue plant never recovered, but it was willingly sacrificed because it brought me a new friend.

Rue graveolens

The name "herb of grace" comes from the holy tradition of using rue sprigs to sprinkle holy water before High Mass. It was also called the "herb of repentence" from the same use. Shakespeare used that symbolism in Hamlet when Ophelia says "There's rue for you and here's some for me; we may call it herb of grace o'Sundays."

At least since the time of ancient Greece, people have thought rue was a powerful defense against witches and evil. Mercury gave Ulysses rue to free him from the witch Circe.

In the Tyrol, bunches of rue and ground ivy were once thought to enable the bearer to see witches. In England young girls made wreathes of rue and willow to foretell marriage or "another year of single blessedness."

It was also considered a powerful healing herb and disinfectant. Brews of rue were taken to improve vision, loosen stiff joints, counteract snake bites and stave off old age. Sprigs of rue were placed on dock benches to protect courts from jail fever.

Today rue is grown primarily as an ornamental or for its symbolism. Italians sometimes use snipped rue leaves in salads and in a little sandwich of walnut kernels between fig halves. The acrid taste and toxic nature of rue, however, discourage most of us from using it for food. Some people are even said to develop a slight skin rash from contact with the leaves.

I have grown rue because it is beautiful, and I'm fascinated by its ancient heritage in mythology, literature and folk tradition.

The leaves are a misty blue-green like moonlight, and the shape of the plant reminds me of a wine glass or tiny elm tree. In midsummer delicate yellow flowers appear, and dried seed pods in the fall are interesting in herb wreathes or dried arrangements.

Rue grows well in rocky, dry, alkaline soil with sun or partial shade. It is a perennial and sometimes even evergreen. Seeds are large and germinate easily. Cuttings usually root well when taken in early summer and kept entirely in shade until well-rooted.

Seed catalogues usually list rue, but remember, ancient Greeks believed rue always grew better when it was stolen.

Sage Advice

Salvia officinalis

From the ancient Latin proverb comes the query. "Cur morietur homo cui Salvia crescit in horto?" (How can a man die who grows sage in his garden?) The very genus name of sage, *Salvia officinalis,* means "health" or "salvation," and the low grey-green plant was once thought to cure almost anything.

Even though sage's role in medicine has waned, its place in cookery is still important. Can you imagine turkey stuffing or pork sausage without a pinch of sage?

In the early Middle Ages sage was added to rich fatty food, like pork, to make digestion easier. That original use of sage has been forgotten and now we use sage to make dishes taste like grandmother's.

Dried sage is a passable substitute for fresh when flavor is the only consideration. For sage's aid in digestion the leaves should be fresh.

A favorite cookbook will describe the traditional uses of sage in poultry and pork. Why not try a pinch of sage in pea soup or sprinkle finely crushed sage over cheese?

To enjoy sage as a healthful tonic, drink sage tea with lemon. The Chinese preferred European sage tea, often trading triple quantity of their choicest native tea for sage.

An enjoyable, exotic drink is sage wine. Following is a variation of an 18th century recipe:

Sage Wine

Combine 1 cup fresh sage leaves and 1 quart good Burgundy. Put in blender on high speed for several minutes. Bottle.

Because sage has been used by so many people for so long, folk truisms abound. Sage promotes a happy home; where sage thrives, the woman rules; sage is a remedy for lethargy or forgetfulness; dark hair rinsed with strong sage tea will stay healthy; and sage as a bath herb is said to soothe tired muscles.

With all these claims, how can you *not* grow sage? A thriving plant should be as necessary to home as the roof.

Find a sunny protected area with plenty of moisture. A rich soil is not vital, but the ground should be kept well-aerated.

Sage seeds are large and germinate easily. Plant them outside in April or at any time inside. In the first season give sage plenty of water and only harvest once. Sage is hardy through almost any winter, but after four or five years the plant gets too woody. It is then time to begin with a new cutting or seedling.

Over a dozen varieties and color variations of sage have been developed by nurseries. It seems to me the white variegated or red tinged sage is the less flavorful and the less winter hardy. This observation may just reflect my own preference because I like plants, like people, to be what they really are.

Whether fancy or plain, sage will reward you with health-promoting savory leaves and a burst of magnificent blue flower spires each spring.

Satureja montana

Hardy winter savory *(Satureja montana)* will bloom long after others have faded. My savory loves the protection of a stone wall. Lacey little flowers and delicate leaves belie the hot, tangy nature of this often overlooked herb. Add the fresh or dried leaves to eggs, all kinds of meat, greens and even butter for a spicy surprise. My children call it the "Pizza plant" because it has the peppery bite reminiscent of pepperoni.

The annual savory *(Satureja hortensis)* is the most widely known savory; if you desire a few ephemeral plants in the vegetable garden, it is the best. Sow savory in early spring; allow four or five weeks for germination; and keep them well weeded for a few more weeks. Savory is said to aid onions, so place the onion patch accordingly.

However, grow winter savory for a little evergreen plant that will grow in worst soil and bloom itself silly. Winter savory seeds are also sown in early spring in a sunny spot. Eventually the roots will spread laterally and the plant can be divided. In the meantime the garden will boast a compact little herb from which fresh leaves may be gathered each day.

Savory was once sprinkled on dishes as parsley is today, and a sprig of savory was traditionally tossed in the pot when beans or peas were cooking. It is said to make these dishes more digestible and less gaseous. Bread crumbs were mixed with savory for breading fish "to give it a quicker rellish."

One of the oldest virtues attributed to both savories is that it will ease the sting of bees. It is true that a shoot of crushed leaves rubbed on an insect sting provides almost instant relief.

Herbalist Culpepper gives an almost endless list of ailments said to be cured by savory. It was thought by the ancients that savory *(satureia)* belonged to the satyrs, and that "Mercury claims the dominion over this herb. Keep it by you all year, if you love yourself and your ease, and it is a hundred pounds to a penny if you do not."

#1: Sweet Marjoram

Origanum majorana

If I could have only one herb on the proverbial desert island, it would be sweet marjoram *(Origanum majorana)*. It was the first plant in my beginner's garden many summers ago, and it has been a mainstay since. I couldn't believe the modest little plant was so sweetly spicy! That first summer I made a potpourri almost entirely of sweet marjoram. My poor husband ate salads with more marjoram than lettuce. My clothes smelled of sweet marjoram from the bunches I hung in the closet. I took marjoram baths and rinsed my hair with marjoram tea.

Thank goodness I eventually recovered and started to appreciate other herbs and more subtle herbal pleasures. But marjoram remains special! Since the Middle Ages it has carried the reputation of spreading happiness.

It is one of the most versatile herbs--don't confuse it with the closely related oregano *(origanum vulgare)*. Sweet marjoram was used abundantly in cooking because of its powers of preserving foods and adding a pleasant taste to food without much flavor of their own.

Finely chopped fresh leaves are especially good with veal, pork or ground beef. Most cooked vegetables benefit from a sprinkle of minced marjoram. This is a good way to use leftover ham:

Leftover Ham

Finely grind twelve ounces of ham and add two tablespoons chopped marjoram, one tablespoon brandy and a little freshly ground pepper. Melt three tablespoons unsalted butter in a pan and add meat mixture. Cook gently for several minutes and then store in the refrigerator for a day before using.

Sweet marjoram is a tender perennial. It is almost impossible to winter it over in our area, so it must be started from seed each spring or carried over the winter in a pot. I take stem cuttings in early August (it roots easily) and keep a windowsill plant until late April when it goes back into the garden. Like most members of the origanum family, sweet marjoram is a native of the Mediterranean region and likes plenty of sun, good drainage and slightly alkaline soil.

The leaves are tiny and light green. Just before it blooms

Good Luck Sesame

Sesamum orientale

Sesame *(Sesamum orientale)* is the good luck plant. Eating the delicious little sesame seeds or just growing the plant in the garden will bring good fortune, according to West African folklore. In the South sesame is known by its African name "benne" because it was first brought to South Carolina by slaves.

Ancient Egyptians ground sesame into a kind of flour. The seeds are so rich that they are often crushed and used as a spread for bread. Sesame oil is known as a drying oil because, like tung oil, it will eventually evaporate instead of remaining liquid like most oils. For this reason sesame oil makes a wonderful cleansing lotion for those with oily skin.

Sesame is best known, however, for its rich flavor in cookies, cake, or bread. The seeds are rich in vitamins C and E, calcium, and unsaturated fatty acids. So sprinkle them liberally on your next loaf of bread. Until sesame seeds are baked or roasted, they are pale and tasteless.

Following is a holiday sesame cookie from a gracious Harpers Ferry lady whose charm and accent are as rich as her cookies.

Peggy Dye's Sesame Cookie

2 cups of brown sugar
1 cup of flour
½ teaspoon baking powder
¼ teaspoon salt
1 beaten egg
¾ cup cooking oil
1 teaspoon vanilla
¾ cups toasted benne seed

Cream the butter and sugar. Add beaten egg and flour sifted with the salt and baking powder. Add vanilla and benne seed. Drop by teaspoon on greased cookie sheets and bake in a 325 oven very quickly. Allow to cool one minute before removing from the pan. This makes a transparent wafer.

Start sesame seedlings inside early enough to give them at least 120 days before frost. Because it is such a heat-loving plant, sesame rarely sets seed in the Blue Ridge area - it is a little too cool. The annual plants, however, are very pretty with slender, dark green leaves and a blossom which looks like foxglove. If the plants are set six inches apart in a sunny spot, they make a bushy border about 18 inches high - bringing a bit of African culture and a lot of good luck.

Romantic, Aromatic Southernwood

Artemisia abrotanum

Southernwood is green and feathery. It is one of the most beautiful plants in the herb garden, and one of the largest of the artemisia family, *(Artemisia abrotanum)*. The foliage is very aromatic and effective in repelling moths and other insects. In fact, in France the herb is called "garde robe."

For years I have grown two large southern-wood shrubs near the entrance to the herb garden where the finely branched leaves can be easily brushed to release their fragrance. Whole hedges of southernwood can be grown if the foliage of this hardy perennial is kept clipped.

Southernwood is a necessity in the weaver's garden or in the garden of anyone who values fine woolens. Fresh branches are hung in closets to discourage moths, and the dried leaves are often tied up in little bags and laid among blankets and sweaters. The scent is always more pleasing than moth balls!

Southernwood's second association is with romance. It was always included in a country lover's bouquet, and its long list of folk names is revealing — Lad and Maiden's Ruin to name a few. Young bo. of burned southernwood leaves on their chins a beard, and bald men once rubbed the ashes on to grow new hair.

Southernwood was used medicinally as a poultic out splinters, and in German the name is *Stub-wurtz* o. herb. Herbalist Turner insists that burning southern will drive away snakes, and Culpepper calls it a "mere plant, worthy of more esteem than it hath.

Among the southernwoods there are three types classifie by their scents: camphor, lemon and tangerine. Lemon and tangerine southernwoods are difficult to find because cuttings seem more difficult to root. The tangerine scent southernwood will grow to seven or eight feet tall and the lemon southernwood has a slightly more grey foliage than the others.

Southernwood will grow in almost any spot with moderately rich soil and full sun. It rarely flowers and almost never sets seed. The best way to propagate the herb is by taking stem cuttings in early summer. They seem to root easily if they are kept out of the sun for a few weeks, and the rooting medium of sand and vermiculite is kept moist. Plants should be spaced four feet apart because southernwood is really a shrub, forming a thick woody base in several years.

We really should resurrect the old tradition of growing southernwood in every dooryard. Following is part of an old Finnish bride song reminding us of southernwood's virtues:

> "I'll give to him
> Who gathers me, more sweetness than
> he'd dream
> Without me—more than any lily could.
> I, that am flowerless, being
> Southernwood."

little round buds are formed at the tips of stems. In fact, it is sometimes called knotted marjoram or choir-boys because of these distinctive knots. Cut back the plants for drying just before these buds open. You will be rewarded with a second harvest during the season, usually the main cutting as the plant will be more bushy the second time around. Marjoram dries easily if spread out on a screen and laid in a dark, dry place like an attic. It is as aromatic when dried, as fresh, and retains its strength for a very long time. Strip the dried leaves from the stems and store them in a cool, dark, dry place in tightly sealed glass jars. Keep the fragrant twigs! They can be hung in closets to freshen clothes or used as sweet-smelling kindling next winter.

Dried marjoram leaves are a good addition to potpourri or bath herbs. Fresh leaves were traditionally used to polish furniture. In the English countryside marjoram tea is enjoyed. The taste is pleasing and it is said to stimulate one's sense of touch. Sweet marjoram water is a mild antiseptic often used to bathe the brow to relieve a headache. Our snuff-dipping ancestors ground sweet marjoram into powder and sniffed it to clear clogged sinuses. Ancient Greeks used it as an antidote for narcotic poisoning.

Sweet marjoram was a particular favorite of the Elizabethans, and that herb-loving Shakespeare knew it well. These lines are from his *All's Well That Ends Well,* Act IV. Scene V:

Lafew: "Twas a good lady, twas a good lady, we may pick a thousand salads ere we light on such another herb."

Clown: "Indeed, sir, she was the sweet marjoram of the salad. . ."

Tanacetum

Tansy: Bitter Passover Herb

New shoots of tansy *(Tanacetum),* looking like bright miniature ferns, poke up in the herb garden just in time for Easter. In England by the 17th century tansy cakes (or tansies) were eaten on Easter to symbolize one of the Bitter Herbs of Passover. It was also thought tansy would strengthen one's health after the sparsities of Lent.

120

Most old recipes for tansies are complicated egg custard concoctions, so at Easter we just sprinkle chopped tansy on our scrambled eggs for a symbolic modern tansy.

Today the beautiful green herb with fine fern-like leaves makes a good background for lower-growing herbs, and it provides us with one of the most effective insect repellants around. Ants and flies abhor its scent! Whole branches are often hung in country pantries or by windows in summer. I stitch up little sachets filled with dried tansy leaves and place them in my cupboards to discourage ants.

So powerful was tansy as an insect repellant and preservative that its name comes from Athanasia, the Greek name for immortality. Dried tansy was often sprinkled on fresh meat to preserve it. Until about 1800 in our country many families laid whole tansy leaves in coffins for both its symbolic connotation and practical embalming qualities.

Tansy has been attributed with hundred of medicinal virtues from "bringing out the measles" to curing one of worms. Just wearing a tansy leaf in your shoe was once thought to prevent ague.

It is a hardy perennial growing to almost four feet. The variety *Tanacetum crispum,* or fernleaf tansy, is smaller and more controllable for gardens, but the pretty yellow flowers are not as profuse. The blossoms grow in clusters called tansy buttons and keep their shape and color perfectly when dried for winter arrangements or herb wreaths.

Grow your tansy against a fence or wall because high winds or rains tend to bend the heavy foliage. It likes full sun to partial shade and any soil that is fairly well-drained. The biggest problem in growing tansy is that it may spread too much. I grow one clump where the lawn mower can keep it under control. The smaller variety I grow in the garden. Since tansy doesn't grow easily from seed, I keep it in bounds by sharing root cuttings each spring.

Rich green foliage, cheerful tansy buttons and the reminder of our entwined heritage make tansy a rewarding herb to grow. May these lines from an old English ballad hold true for you.

"On Easter Sunday be the pudding seen, To which the Tansy lends her sober green."

Tarragon - the Little Dragon

Tarragon *(Artemisia dracunculus)* is ready for the first harvest in the herb garden by May. The bushy, grey-green perennial plant has grown more than a foot tall, and all but two or three inches of the stems may be safely cut.

It was once thought that tarragon did not dry well, and if not used fresh, could only be preserved in vinegar. However, Mrs. Adelma Simmons' (Caprilands Herb Farm in Connecticut) method works well. She suggests using the first harvest for drying and the second harvest in August for making vinegar.

Artemisia dracunculus

Spread the newly cut tarragon thinly in a shallow basket and let it dry in a shady spot. When crispy, store it in a tall jar so the leaves are not disturbed. Crumble the leaves as they are used. Most herbs store better if left whole until used.

Tarragon Vinegar

It is important to use a high quality white wine vinegar so the delicate tarragon taste is not overpowered. Fill a jar as full as possible with tarragon cuttings and pour the vinegar over them. Close the jar and keep it in a warm dark place for several weeks. Strain the vinegar with cheesecloth and replace it in the jar with a fresh sprig of tarragon for decoration and identification.

Tarragon vinegar on salad or in making deviled eggs is delicious. Fresh tarragon is the "secret" ingredient in Bernaise sauce. More simply, add a pinch of tarragon to mayonnaise for summer salads that include seafood or eggs. Try sprinkling fresh chopped tarragon on broiled fish, chicken or tomatoes.

Tarragon comes from Siberia and was first mentioned by the Greeks about 500 B.C. as a "simple"(a one-herb remedy) used by Hippocrates. During the Middle Ages, it was grown in monestary gardens in France and finally came to England during the time of the Tudors. For a long time it was grown only in royal gardens and was almost a symbol of nobility. By the early 19th century, however, it was growing in America.

The name tarragon is a corruption of the French Estragon and means "little dragon." Variations of this warlike name are used by many countries, but I have not been able to discover its origin.

Never buy tarragon seeds! If it flowers and sets seed, it is not true French tarragon, but a close Russian relative without the wonderful aroma taste which makes tarragon so valued. Tarragon has been so domesticated that it will not reproduce itself. Cuttings must be taken for propagation. Dividing the roots of a mature plant or taking stem cuttings is the usual way to propogate tarragon. Fortunately it roots easily in moist sandy soil. but not in direct sunlight.

Tarragon grows best with partial shade and a richer, more moist soil than most herbs, but it will not tolerate poor drainage. It will be happy with a summer mulch of peat moss and a winter mulch of straw. Tarragon seems to need a little fertilizer during the growing season; it is one of the few herbs whose flavor is not diminished by a rich soil.

The roots seem to spread out a foot or so from the plant, so be careful with the hoe. Remember to plant the inside tarragon in a container with a minimum of ten inches to accommodate the sprawling root system.

Because tarragon has such a long and cherished history, its folklore is rich. It was thought to increase stamina simply by being worn in the bottom of shoes. As a simple, it was used to strengthen the heart, lungs and liver.

The ancients cautioned us to avoid using tarragon alone in a salad but to combine it with "Lettuce, Purslain, and Rocket." Gerard in 1633 writes about "many strange tales scarce worth noting, saying, that the seed of flax put into a radish roote or Sea Onion and so set, doth bring forth this herbe Tarragon." Let me know if it works!

Thyme: Dawn in Paradise

The tiniest herb patch is never complete without thyme - the classic herb. Literature is filled with descriptions of banks of thyme, walks of thyme, sundials surrounded with thyme and whole thyme lawns. Its fragrance has been described as "dawn in paradise."

Thyme comes in dozen of varieties. The taller eight-to-ten inch kind is called *Thymus vulgaris,* and the low mat-forming thyme is *Thymus serpylum* (sometimes commonly called mother-of-thyme). Among these two larger groups are dozens of varieties. Some herb gardeners make an interesting hobby of just growing thymes. There is a thyme which smells like lemon *(Thymus serpyllum vulgaris enmodora);* a thyme which smells and tastes like caraway *(Thymus herbs barona)· Thymus lanculis* is a wooly thyme; the golden-leaved thyme *(Thymus serpyllum arneus);* and thymes with silver leaves *(Thymus serpyllum argentensa).* The list could go on for pages.

Thymus vulgaris

But all of these delicate little plants are ancient symbols of energy and magic. Bees with their feverish activity have been associated with thyme since before recorded history. On summer days, my bed of thyme is literally alive with bees hovering above the delicate pink blossoms.

Medieval ladies embroidered their scarves with a bee and a sprig of thyme for presentation of knights going into battle. Little bushes of thyme were planted on graves in Wales and even today some secret fraternal societies use thyme in graveside ceremonies.

The finest honey is thyme honey. Orchards were traditionally planted with ground-covers of thyme to attract bees and insure pollination for the fruit trees.

Thyme is one of the herbs always included in the Christmas manger scene as legend records it was in the hay of the Christ Child's bed. Almost every old charm designed to enable one to see the fairies and wood elves included thyme. In fact the fairies are said to lay their sleeping babies in the tiny cradle-shaped thyme blossoms.

The virtues of thyme are as varied as its fame. Medi-

124

cinally, it was used in a tea to ease a cough, strengthen eyesight, soothe an upset stomach and "remove headaches occasioned by inebriation." Thymol is a commercially valuable product of thyme oil which is effective as a germicide.

Thyme gives a pleasant taste to red meat, seafood and poultry. Sprinkle dried or fresh thyme on the meat before cooking, or add thyme to stuffings for poultry or veal. It is indispensable to cooks for bouquet garni. For sauces, thyme is added during the cooking - always sparingly and often in the form of a whole sprig which can be removed before the sauce is completed.

Even hearty vegetables like onions or tomatoes benefit from a bit of thyme. Try this recipe when the garden beans are ready to harvest.

Green Beans and Thyme

Cook a pound of fresh cut green beans for five minutes. Drain well. Heat 4 tablespoons of butter, a tablespoon of olive oil, 4 tablespoons of fresh thyme and a crushed garlic clove. Add the beans and toss together with a little pepper and a tablespoon of grated Parmesan cheese.

Thyme is most easily grown by dividing clumps of established plants or by taking stem cuttings in early summer. Since thyme seeds are so tiny and the seedlings are so delicate, start seeds indoors. Germination takes place in two weeks; and seedlings will be ready to set out in four weeks. Set nine inches apart in a sunny, well-drained location. Make sure the soil is very fine and that weeds are kept out for the first season. The thick roots of a thyme bed seem to deplete the soil quickly, so add a little compost each year after the second season. By mulching with straw, the plants should winter-over well in the Blue Ridge. Thyme is one of the last herbs to green up in spring, so do not panic if new growth does not appear until May.

Thyme is one of the easiest herbs to harvest, dry and store. Cut it back to two or three inches once in midsummer. Spread the stems and leaves out on a screen in a warm, dark and dry place. When they are crispy, rub the tiny leaves through the screen onto clean newspaper. Store in airtight jars in a cool, dry place. Be sure to dry some whole sprigs for cooking or other important uses such as the one described in this old English song:

"O I was a damsel so fair.
But fairer I wished to appear.
So I washed me in milk, and
I dressed me in silk.
And put the sweet thyme in my hair."

Woodruff Scents the Sheets

Asperula odorata

Springtime in the herb garden means sweet woodruff *(Asperula odorata)* with its glossy dark green leaves and tiny white blossoms. It carpets the forest floor of its native Germany and was brought to our country by early settlers.

In late April, just in time to make May wine, sweet woodruff pushes up whorls of leaves like the spokes of a small wheel. The first time the herb appeared in print, in the 13th century, it was called "wuderove" from the French "rovelle" for wheel.

It is the traditional flavoring in May wine, and for me the rich smell of sweet woodruff is the essence of high spring. Make your May wine to celebrate May Day and the beginning of another growing season. Heat three or four leaves of sweet woodruff in the oven until the scent is strong and then steep them in a gallon of Rhine wine for a week. To be really festive, serve the flavored wine half and half with champagne, and garnish it with a fresh West Virginia Johnny-jump-up.

Fresh sweet woodruff has a mild woodsy scent, and only when dried is the wonderful smell of vanilla and new mown hay released. This is because it contains coumarin, a fixative often used to blend and hold other herb scents.

During the Middle Ages dried sweet woodruff was hung in churches and used in bouquets with lavender and roses to decorate the altar on St. Peter's or St. Barnabas' Day. School children a century ago liked to press the leaves between the pages of their books for the sweet smell, and elegant dandies often kept a dried whorl in their watch cases.

Today it is used to stuff small pillows to keep among

sheets and linens, and is often included in potpourri. In Germany, where it is called Waldmeister, the leaves are sometimes stored in brandy to use all year long for flavoring drinks.

My sweet woodruff grows happily under a dogwood tree and in the shade of a nearby fence. It is one of the few herbs which need shade and slightly acidic soil. As a ground cover for shady areas or under trees, it is beautiful. Starry circles of eight long oval leaves grow out from a center stem with tiny hairs. The delicate white flowers are also stars with four petals. The whole plant never grows taller than six inches. Make sure to leave the lowest foliage when you cut sweet woodruff.

Since the seeds are almost impossible to germinate, often taking up to a year, it is best to buy the first plant. After the initial season, the herb will naturally spread, and you can help it along by taking root divisions. Although sweet woodruff likes moist soil, it also needs good drainage and a loose soil. Recreating its native forest floor of leaf mold is best, but I have found it will spread quickly and thrive if peat moss is mixed generously with the soil.

Grow sweet woodruff, and as herbalist John Gerard instructed us in 1633, use it

> ". . .made up into garlands or bundles
> and hanged up in houses in the heate of
> summer, it doth very wel temper the aire,
> coole and make fresh the place, to the delight
> and comfort of such as are therin."

BIBLIOGRAPHY

Beston, Henry, *Herbs and the Earth.* Doubleday Doran and Co., New York, 1935.

Brown, Alice Cooke, *Early American Herb Recipes.* Charles E. Tuttle Co., Tokyo, 1966.

Clarkson, Rosetta I., *Herbs and Savory Seeds.* Dover Publishing Co., Dover, New York, 1972. (Also known as *Magic Gardens,* MacMillan, 1940.)
―――――― *The Golden Age of Herbs and Herbalists.* Dover Publishing Co., New York, 1972. (Also known as *Green Enchantment,* MacMillan, 1940)

Doole, Louise Evans, *Herb Magic and Garden Craft.* Sterling Publishing Co., New York, 1972.

Earle, Alice Morse, *Sundials and Roses of Yesterday.* Charles E. Tuttle Co., Rutland, Vermont, 1902.

Fettner, Ann Tucker, *Potpourri.* Workman Publishing Co., New York, 1977.

Flint, Martha Bockee, *A Garden of Simples.* Scribners, New York, 1900.

Foley, Daniel, *Herbs for Use and Delight.* (An Anthology from the Herbarist) Dover Publishing Co., New York, 1974.

Fox, Helen Morgantheau, *Herb Gardening with Herbs for Flavor and Fragrances.* Dover Publishing Co., New York, 1970.

Freeman, Margaret B., *Herbs for the Medieval Household.* New York Metropolitan Museum of Art, 1943.

Grieve, M., *Culinary Herbs and Condiments.* Dover Publishing Co., New York, 1971.

Horton, Julia F., *Herbs and Spices.* Golden Press, New York, 1976.

Howarth, Sheila, *Herbs With Everything.* Holt, Rinehart and Winston, New York, 1976.

Kamm, Minnie Watson, *Old Time Herbs for Northern Gardens.* Dover Publishing Co., 1971.

Krutch, Joseph, *Herbal.* David R. Godine, Boston 1965.

Leighton, Ann, *Early American Gardens "For Meate or medicine."* Houghton Mifflin Co., Boston, 1970.

——————— *American Gardens of the 18th Century.* Houghton Mifflin Co., Boston, 1976.

Lucas, Richard, *The Magic of Herbs in Daily Living.* Parker Publishing Co., New York, 1972.

Lust John, *The Herb Book.* Bantam, New York, 1974.

Mawson, Monica, *Herb and Spice Cookery.* Hamlyn, Toronto, 1970.

Meyer, Joseph E., *The Herbalist.* Rand McNally, London, 1918 (Revised in 1960).

Miller, Amy Bess, *Shaker Herbs, a History And Compendium.* Clarkson N. Potter, New York, 1976.

Northcote, Lady Rosalind, *The Book of Herb Lore.* Dover, Publishing Co., New York, 1971.

Reppert, Bertha P., *A Heritage of Herbs.* Stackpole, Harrisburg, Pa., 1976.

Rodale, *Rodale Herb Book.* Rodale Press, Emmaus, Pa., 1974.

Rohde, Elinor Sinclair, *The Old English Herbals.* Dover Publishing Co., New York, 1971. (Also, Longman, Green and Company. 1922).

Simmons, Adelma G., *Herb Gardening in Five Seasons.* Hawthorne, New York, 1964.

Simmons, Adelma G., *Herb Gardens of Delight.* Hawthorne, New York, 1974.

de Sounin, Leonie, *Magic in Herbs.* Gramercy Publishing Co., New York, 1961.

Sunset Book, *How to Grow Herbs.* Lane Publishing Co., California, 1970.

Primary Sources

Culpepper, Nicholas, *The English Physician.* S. Ballard, R. Ware, et al London, 1741.

Gerarde, John, *The Herball or Generall Historie of Plantes,* edited by Thomas Jonson. Norton and Whitakers, London, 1633.

Parkinson, John, *Paradisi in Sole.* Methven and Co., 1904, Reprinted from 1621 Edition.

Credits: Woodcut illustrations of herbs in compendium taken from John Gerard's *Herbal*, 1633. Dover Publications, Inc., New York.

Cover Photo: Harold Chamblin

INDEX

A

Africa, 116-117
Agrimony, 11
Alchemilla alpina, 98
Alchemilla vulgaris, 97
Allicin, 91
Allium liliaceae, 90
Allium schoenoprasum, 84
Allspice, 71
Amish, 23
Angelica, 18,103
Angelica archangelica, 18, 64
Anchovy and tarragon spread, 27
Anise, 3,57
Anthanasia, 121
Anthemis nobilis, 81
Anthriscus cerefolium, 83
Apples, 71
Apollo, 75
Aristotle, 25
Artemis (Diana), 55
Artemisia, 8, 12, 21, 55, 64, 67
Artemisia annua, 66
Artemisia abrotanum, 55, 117
Artemisia absinthium, 55
Artemisia dracunulus, 55, 122
Artemisia vulgaris, 38,55
Ash, 28, 64
Asperula odorota, 126
Austria, National Library, 5

B

Bacon, Sir Francis, 80
Bancke, 5
Bartram, John, 76, 78
Basil, 3, 16, 18, 26, 34, 41-42
    47, 59, 66, 75-76
Bay leaf, 3-4, 11, 34, 46, 63, 67
    70, 74
Baucis, 71
Beans, - tonka 46, vanilla 46
Bee bread, 79
Bee hive, 14
Bee skep, 14
Bee balm, 23, 28, 50, 68, 76
    77-78
Bees, 38, 70, 79, 96, 103, 124

Belle Grove Plantation, 18
Benne, 57, 116
Bergamot, 3, 8, 16, 21, 23, 34
    48, 77-78
Beston, Henry, 4
Beverages, 3, 12, 26, 36-38
    47, 75, 77-78, 88, 102
    104. 126
Bible, 15, 25, 37, 68, 86, 96
Birdbaths, 14
Birds, 66
Bishop's Garden, Washington
    Cathedral, 17
Bittersweet, 64
Bladderwrack, 11
Blue Ridge, 18, 37, 66, 74
    77, 79, 89, 95-96, 103
    106
Blue Salvia, 34
Books,
    Book of Days, 63
    Garden of Simples, 6
    Godey's Lady's Book, 56
    Goodman of Paris, 74
    Grete Herbal, 5
    Herball, 5
    Herbs and the Earth, 4
    Leech Book of Bald, 5
    Paradisi in Sole, 6
    Papyrus Ebrus, 5
Borago officinalis, 78
Borage, 3-4, 20, 28, 30, 34
    38, 41-42, 49, 59, 61,
    78-79
Borland, Hal, 46
Bouquet garni, 4, 125
Boxwood, 67, 70
Bread, 27, 56-57, 85, 88,
    115-116
Breath fresheners, 88
Brooklyn Botanical Gardens, 13
Burnet, 79-80
Burra, 78
Butter, 27, 79, 83, 85, 103, 115

C

Calendula, 8, 16, 18, 28, 34, 42
    49, 53, 61, 100, 109

131

F

Feast of Passover, 95
Featherfew, 34, 82, 89, 90
Fennel, 3-4, 18, 47, 86-88
Fern, 11, 23
Fertilizer, 19-20, 32, 41, 66, 84
Flint, Martha, 6
Florence Fennel, 7, 88
Fines Herbes, 3
Finland, 90
Finocchio, 88
Fish, 3, 83, 88, 122, 125
Fishing charms, 94
Fixatives, 54, 68, 71, 126
Foeniculum vulgare, 87
Folklore, 11, 20, 23-25, 28-29
    36-38, 61-64, 68, 70-71
    74-75, 77, 80
Foxglove, 62
France, 11, 83, 96-97, 117, 122-
    123
Frankincense, 70
Furniture polish, 53, 120
Fernleaf tansy, 121

G

Gaelic, 11
Garde robe, 55, 117
Garden of Simples, 6
Gardener, Mayster Ion, 108 108
Gardens, 8-9, 11-13, 15-20, 28
    77-78, 97-98
Garlic. 3-4, 38, 67, 90
Gerard, John, 4-5, 25, 39, 62
    74, 84, 90, 93-95, 123, 127
Geranium
    lemon rose, 12, 92
    lime, 92
    mint, 92
    nutmeg, 12
    rose, 50, 92
    scented, 10, 12, 34, 41
        53, 59, 92-93
Germander, 18, 66
Germany, 118, 126
Ginger, 3, 23, 71
Godey's Lady's Book, 56
Goodman of Paris, 74
Grapefruit, 71

Greek, 31, 64, 70, 75, 76-78
    82, 86, 88, 107, 109, 111-
    113, 120-122
Grete Herbal, 74
Guatemala, 100
Guy Mannering, 64
Gypsies, 29

H

Halloween, 67, 75
Harpers Ferry, 14, 16, 18, 42
    69, 96
Hawthorne, 31
Hefner Publishing, 5
Hen and chicks, 93-94
Hemlock, 28
Herba Luisa, 101
Herbe aux Chat, 80
Herbs
    annual, 8, 18, 22, 26, 41
        66, 75, 77, 79, 82-83, 88
        109, 115, 117
    bath, 10-11, 77, 120
    biennial, 87, 107
    compendium, 73-127
    cosmetics, 12, 82, 96, 102
        116
    Drying, 33, 52-54, 76-77
        79, 81-82, 85, 97, 100
        102-103, 105-106, 108, 110
        120, 125
    flavoring, 2, 36, 37
    growth requirements (soil,
        light, cultivation, water) 12
        16-20, 22, 32, 40-41, 59-60
        66, 74-75, 78-79, 81-84
        87-89, 93, 95, 97-101, 103
        105-106, 108, 110-111,113
        -115, 117-119, 121, 123
        125, 127
    harvesting, 33-34, 51, 74
        77, 82, 85-86, 90, 106, 115
        120, 122, 125
    Italian, 42-43-44
    medicinal, 11, 23-25, 28-29
        36-37, 47, 53, 62, 68
        77, 79, 81-83, 86,90-92
        94-95, 99, 101, 103, 106-
        107, 109, 111-112, 115
        118, 120-121, 124

134

Herbs are a way of life for author Linda Rago, who in this excellent year - round guide, shares her knowledge and love of herbs. Mrs. Rago is a sensitive writer with an easy and comfortable style — a delightful way with words!

For those who love to cook and eat well, there are favorite recipes and a wealth of ideas for using herbs each month of the year. In addition, *Dooryard Herbs* expresses the author's special fascination for history and herbal lore.

Linda lives with her husband Ron and children Reid and Jane in a charming mid-nineteenth century house in Harpers Ferry, West Virginia.

A frequent contributor to newspapers and magazines, the author has written a weekly newspaper column on herbs and an article for *Country Magazine.*

Dooryard Herbs is further enhanced by the original pen and ink drawings of illustrator Evalina Manucy Stowell, a Harpers Ferry artist who has illustrated *Meet the Craftsman.* Mrs. Stowell, also an herb gardener, is co-owner of Stowell Galleries in Harpers Ferry and Directoress of the Harpers Ferry Montessori School.

This book is set in
11 point Press Roman type,
printed by
STUDIO 20
Frederick, Maryland
on 70# Mohawk Vellum Paper
1984